P9-AGA-398

# Crossing the Internet Threshold

## An Instructional Handbook

**Roy Tennant**

**John Ober**

**Anne G. Lipow**

Foreword by Clifford A. Lynch

Library Solutions Press

First Edition. Third printing; revised.

An earlier version of this book was published as a workbook in support of hands-on Internet training workshops.

*Designed by Roy Tennant*

Sales Office:      1100 Industrial Road, Suite 9, San Carlos, CA 94070
                   $45.00.  Inquire about discounts for quantity orders.
Editorial Office: 2137 Oregon Street, Berkeley, CA 94705
                   510-841-2636; Fax: 510-841-2926

ISBN  1-882208-01-3        Printed and bound in the United States of America.

Software, computer and product names mentioned in *Crossing the Internet Threshold: An Instructional Handbook* are for identification purposes only and may be trademarks of their respective companies. Mention in this book does not imply endorsement.

# Table of Contents

## H. Trainer's Aids

## I. Appendix

## J. Index

# Notes

# Foreword by Clifford A. Lynch

Members of the information services community are hearing constantly that the Internet — or the National Research and Education Network (NREN), or whatever one chooses to call the developing global web of computer communications networks — is vitally important to the future of librarians, libraries and information services. There is no doubt in anyone's mind that it will have a revolutionary impact on communications among researchers and professionals in a wide variety of disciplines.

The Internet is now a place to disseminate information, to seek information, to communicate, to teach and to learn, and to conduct business and commerce. But for those not yet part of this dynamic, rapidly growing medium, pathways across the Internet threshold have been somewhat mysterious and hard to identify. Yet there is no substitute for being there. Those who only perceive the Internet and its capabilities second hand may believe it to be both less and more than it really is. Expectations about the Internet probably parallel and repeat expectations about many types of information technology that have appeared over the past decade, such as personal computers and online catalogs, among those yet to gain direct experience with them. Those looking in from the outside tend to expect the capabilities of the technology to be superior to the actual state of the art. Personal computer software is still amazingly crude, and online catalogs are still not nearly as easy to use or as helpful as one might wish. So it is with the Internet. Much of the network access software is downright savage, and effective navigational tools are still largely nonexistent — though a lot of smart people are working on these problems, and the situation improves every day. A novice approaching the network with a vision derived from the popular media or from science fiction authors such as William Gibson, who have written about the future of the network, will be greatly disappointed and perhaps puzzled. At the same time, crude as all this technology is, even those of us who have been deeply involved with the technology and are as comfortable as anyone can be with the current state of the art, tend to underestimate the sweeping social and organizational changes that the new technologies are introducing. Perhaps those most familiar tend to be the most oblivious because they are too close to the technology.

The promise of the Internet and the developing set of tools that allow us to access and navigate Internet resources also challenge us with the need for a massive training and retraining program for library and information professionals, as well as a more broadly based program for the general user community. This book is part of the response to that challenge.

*Crossing the Internet Threshold* can be viewed as a user's manual of the Internet for the beginning user. In a real sense, it's a survival guide. While the information contained here is generally applicable, the examples are particularly oriented to the interests of librarians and information professionals. There is also a great deal here that will be helpful to people developing training seminars similar to those for which the material here was first prepared.

## Foreword
### cont'd

This book does not contain a detailed explanation of how all the technology involved in the Internet works. In fact, it treats this technology in only the most superficial way and provides a few pointers towards more detailed information. I think this emphasis affirms that the Internet is beginning to mature as a vehicle that offers valuable services to its users rather than as an end unto itself. While there are those who are interested in the technology of how things work, most people do not need or want to understand the details of electrical power generation and distribution just to plug in an appliance; nor are they concerned with the intricacies of internal combustion engine engineering in order to drive or ride in a car. In the same sense, this book is concerned with how to *use* the Internet to communicate and to find information.

It's interesting to note that all three of the authors of this book are (among many other things) teachers. However, at least two of the three authors have done most of their teaching not in the traditional academic faculty context but in the rather different context of bibliographic instruction — a very pragmatically oriented form of teaching which focuses on allowing information seekers to select and use appropriate tools rather than on the theory and practice of how to design those tools. It seems to me particularly appropriate to see this same approach applied to a guide to getting started on the Internet, and it is a perspective which I believe readers will appreciate.

One of the great difficulties of the Internet is that the set of available tools and services can vary greatly, depending on where you are and how you connect to it. Sitting in an office with a high-end workstation and a direct connection at a major university offers one view of the world. There is a different view for a person in a small library, with a fairly modest PC, who is trying to access resources on the Internet using a modem. In the early days of the Internet, the focus was on the first of these two scenarios. Today, there are a number of programs that are oriented towards opening up the Internet to more and more users. I was particularly pleased to see that this book covers the issues faced by such new users, and even users-to-be trying to find out how to get connected.

It's very important, I believe, to make the effort to familiarize more people with the world of the Internet and the developing networked information revolution. These forces, over the next decade or so, will have massive effects on publishing, scholarly communication, teaching and learning, access to government information and other areas of our lives. And they may not be the effects that we are expecting or assuming. Without some firsthand knowledge of what lies beyond the Internet threshold, it will be hard for us to conduct informed discussion about how we want our institutions, activities, and public policies to evolve in an age of global connectivity and networked information.

*Clifford A. Lynch is Director of Library Automation for the University of California.*

CROSSING THE INTERNET THRESHOLD

# A | Preface

*This section contains:*

- About This Book
- Acknowledgements
- About the Authors

# About This Book

This book is addressed to two categories of reader: the person who has access to the Internet and wants to learn how to take advantage of its vast resources; and the person who wants to teach Internet skills to others. The predecessor of this first edition was a "workshop edition" that we prepared in support of a 14-hour institute in which participants each worked at their own terminal. With the workshop edition for ready reference, plus a combination of lecture, demonstration, exercises (for both beginners and advanced level students), and discussion, participants were able to assimilate information about the Internet on both the practical and conceptual levels. This handbook attempts to preserve that dual-level potential: it includes the content of the institute lectures and the beginning and advanced level exercises, as well as discussion topics, sample overheads and other materials, and a checklist of reminders that trainers will find useful.

Expecting that many readers would not read the book from cover to cover, but instead jump to the pages that interested them at the moment, we repeated some information in different chapters so that each chapter could stand alone.

We would like to think that this handbook will be useful over time. But the Internet — its technology, size, content, its very definition — is changing so rapidly that you can be sure some of the information in this book was out of date the day after it was put into print.

Do not be concerned if a particular procedure or step-by-step instruction in the book doesn't work in your environment. There are a variety of ways that you may access and use the Internet. Our aim in this book is to explain clearly and concisely the "lowest common denominator" methods of using the Internet. What is covered herein will, by and large, work for everyone who can logon to an Internet-connected computer. When we cite commands or strategies that are specific to a particular situation (for example, the UNIX operating system), we try to make that clear. If your situation allows you to use more sophisticated software to accomplish file transfer, remote connections, and electronic mail, then by all means use them. For many readers, however, the methods covered in this book are the ones they will need to use.

Whether we were successful in our goal to provide both a useful introductory resource for neophytes and a guide for trainers, all of whom may be using different operating systems and a countless variety of access software, only you, the user of this handbook, can judge. We welcome your suggestions for improving it and, of course, want to know what you find useful. And we certainly hope you will call our attention to any errors you spot. Please write to us:

c/o    Library Solutions Institute
2137 Oregon Street
Berkeley, CA 94705

or contact Anne Lipow via e-mail: alipow@library.berkeley.edu

# Acknowledgements

**The authors** wish to thank the staff at UC Berkeley for their comments on the earliest version of the Workshop Edition. The present volume incorporates many of their suggestions for change. Also, while the authors take full responsibility for any errors or lack of clarity, the book is a far better one for having undergone the close scrutiny of Clifford Lynch and Glee Willis.

**Roy Tennant** wishes to thank Glee Willis for being the best "net buddy" a guy could hope to have, De Stanton for contributing more than she will admit to, Cathy Dinnean for graphics advice, David Robison and the Library Technology Watch Program for information and encouragement, Charles W. Bailey, Jr. for leading the way, and Gina Cuclis for more than would fit on these pages.

**John Ober** would like to thank the MLIS students of UC Berkeley who attended the Spring, 1992 Seminar on Networks and Networked Information for their enthusiasm and willingness to experiment. He also wishes to thank Cisco and Poncho and acknowledge the music of Marc Cohn and the Indigo Girls for keeping him entertained.

**Anne G. Lipow** is indebted to Paul Payne and Angeline Lok for their years of unwavering technical support; to Laine Farley and Roy Tennant for their unfailing ability to translate highly technical concepts so she can sort of understand them, and for believing that anyone who asks them the same question three times is perfectly normal; to Bill Whitson and Alan Ritch, from whom she has learned a lot about online searching and how to teach it to others; and to the UC Berkeley Library staff, who taught her most of what she knows about training.

# About the Authors

**Roy Tennant** is the Public Service Automated Systems Coordinator and the Coordinator of Library Instruction at the University of California, Berkeley Library. Roy is also a commercial whitewater river guide and has led trips down numerous western rivers, including the Colorado River through the Grand Canyon.

**John Ober** has been a professor in the School of Library and Information Studies, University of California, Berkeley, since 1987. He also holds degrees in English and Studies of the Future. He designed and instituted a graduate course in Networks and Networked Information in 1992. He has been named an American Library Association Library Book Fellow, travelling to Benin, West Africa, for 1992-1993. When not focusing on issues of the management of information technology you may find him cross-country bicycling or scuba diving.

**Anne G. Lipow** is a training and management consultant to libraries, and founder and director of the Library Solutions Institute, a vehicle for small-group deliberations about issues on the cutting edge of the profession. She is a frequent speaker, author, and workshop presenter in areas of staff development and organizational change. Formerly, she was Director of Instructional Services at the University of California, Berkeley, Library. As a co-owner of The Dreidel Factory, she may be the world's only manufacturer of a hand-made wooden dreidel (a 4-sided top used for celebrating Channukah).

# Notes

# B | Internetworking Overview

*This section contains:*

- Introduction to Networking
- Names and Addresses
- Evolution of Networks & Network Services

# Introduction to Networking

## Introduction

It is valuable to have a basic understanding of what computer networking and internetworking involves before and during your use of the Internet. This grounding will provide a conceptual framework upon which to build and expand your understanding not just of the technology but of the tasks you can accomplish with the technology. It may help you understand what has happened when things go wrong. It should help you understand and participate in discussions about the probable future of the Internet and the appropriate uses of Internet resources. It will help you place in context the new vocabulary and practical knowledge that the rest of this book tries to deliver. This section attempts to give you some of that understanding. It is only a first approximation, delivered from the authors' experience in answering questions about what the Internet is and how it works to both new and experienced Internet users.

Networking is a simple idea: the sharing of expensive resources among computer users. These resources may be the computers themselves, databases (for example, of bibliographic holdings), printers, or even of human expertise. In each case, rather than duplicate the resource or transport it, the resource is provided to a user who may be some distance away via connections between computers. Though the idea is simple, its implementation is quite complex. To connect computers and transfer data and information successfully between them requires a set of rules, or protocols. Just as human communication depends upon rules — students raise their hands to receive permission to speak, for example — The Internet protocols, usually referred to as the TCP/IP (Transmission Control Protocol/Internet Protocol) suite, are documented in thousands of pages of material (see the *Fact Sheet* "Requests For Comments"). However, as with other complex technologies, whether automobiles or video-cassette recorders, new users can be given metaphors and overview perspectives that increase their understanding without overburdening them with technological details.

## Useful Metaphors

The Internet has been described using several different metaphors. Considered as a type of "highway" system, the focus is on the pathways between computers and on the destinations or resources available. Similarly, it has been referred to as an ocean upon which you may take a trip or a cruise, but which must be navigated in order to find your way. Navigational tools, both printed finding aids and computer programs, are necessary for the traveller.

The authors are fond of an architectural metaphor — the Internet as a special building or dwelling — to communicate ideas about the structure and use of the Internet. Thus one finds a certain set of activities available in the "electronic mail room" and another set of activities devoted to the "remote login" room, and must pay attention to a sense of location in order to successfully use the facilities of the building. Of course it is with some boldness and perhaps trepidation as well that one first crosses the Internet threshold.

**Useful Perspectives**

When learning about the Internet or when using it, it will be helpful to consider that any network simultaneously has components which are:

*Technological* – how does it work?

*Social/political* – who makes it work, who uses it?

*Functional* – what can be done with it?

*Technological Perspective*

What do you need to know about the technological pieces of networks? You may live quite comfortably in your house without knowing, in detail, about the materials with which it was constructed or the rules, such as electrical codes, under which it was built. But you are aware enough to distinguish a roof leak from a plumbing leak, or a dripping faucet from a broken refrigerator. These basic distinctions and vocabulary help you describe the house, talk to repair workers, and plan for its future. The basic technical distinctions and vocabulary of networking are important for the same reasons. While our purpose here is not to give a data communications tutorial, it is important to sketch some of the technological landscape.

We often think of the technology primarily as hard, or touchable, components — computers, modems, routers, and transmission media — which are in the technician's domain. However, there are two fundamental distinctions and frequently-used terms that should be in the user's domain as well: *speed* and *information organization*.

In networking terms, *speed*, or capacity, of a link between computers partially determines how quickly an exchange takes place and how much total electronic traffic the network can accommodate. Current speeds range from a relatively slow 56 thousand bits per second (kilobits per second - Kbps) to 45 million bits per second (megabits per second - Mbps - the speed of "T3" links). Speeds in the billions of bits per second (gigabits per second - Gbps) are coming into use. An awareness of the relative speed and capacity of a link will enable you to predict or explain some variance in response time of a computer.

*Organization of information* refers to the "units" that the communicating computers can exchange — messages, files, or at a more fundamental level packets and datagrams — and to the tools with which users locate important information, such as directories. Some network protocols operate on a very limited definition of the unit that can be exchanged, for example FTP is for files only. Others limit the size of the unit exchanged, for example, e-mail messages may have a maximum length.

The technology also consists of the soft or untouchable components, by which we mean the rules and protocols which are embedded in network and application software. From this technological perspective it may be helpful to distinguish between a set of well-defined rules, such as the TCP/IP protocol suite, or the OSI "model" protocols, and a particular piece of software that implements them. Though they follow the same rules, in terms of what they accomplish, two pieces of software may appear quite differently to the user. This explains some of the variance among, for example, Telnet implementations, and why the authors of guides like this one should carefully identify differences between generic capabilities and specific implementations.

The most important feature of this soft technology perspective for the new Internet user concerns the rules and conventions in naming machines and users. Just as you identify your house with a postal address, so too must you have an address on the Internet. In fact, all machines, services, and users "on the net" have an address (see the *Names and Addresses* section of this chapter for further details). Of course, when mail gets delivered it must take a certain path, or route, to its destination. The routing of network traffic is a deeper level of the soft technology.

### Social/Political Perspective

The amazing technological feat of using a computer whose location may be across the world from you may obscure the social and political components of a network. Of course, the communication habits among *users* — as individuals collaborate in new ways, or as groups of people create electronic forums of discussion — are immediately obvious to the new network user and much discussed among network observers and participants. Other groups of people contribute to network development and operation, and those groups negotiate, make compromises, and strike bargains internally and with other groups. This is particularly true of *standards makers* who operate at the international (for example, the International Standards Organization - ISO), national (for example the National Information Standards Organization - NISO), and local level as well as in subject specific areas (for example, the American Library Association Committee on Representation in Machine-Readable Form of Bibliographic Information - MARBI).

Another important group of people document and evaluate the network and the resources available. This is becoming a daunting task, as the number of machines, people, and resources quickly expands. There are worries that the *documenters and evaluators* cannot keep pace with the expansion, in part because many of them altruistically produce manuals, guides, and directories in their "spare" time.

Finally, coming full circle, there are the technologists themselves. Those who design, prototype, and operate network software and hardware are engaged not only in technical cooperation of various sorts, but also in local, national, and international efforts to secure funding, develop technological priorities, and affect public policy relating to technology. *Systems administrators, programmers, network experimenters* (who are represented in the *Fact Sheets*), and *vendors* form this group. It should come as no surprise that they often are the main players in the support groups, or network advocacy groups, such as the Coalition for Networked Information or the Electronic Frontier Foundation.

## Functional Perspective

Networks also can be distinguished from each other by their differing capabilities. One network may be capable of delivering messages but not of interactive connection; such is the case of the BITNET network. Another network, such as the Internet, may be capable of a quite full range of functions. Of course, these functional differences are reflected in the protocols and arise, in part, from the processing capabilities of machines themselves.

The Internet has three main capabilities: messaging, remote login, and file exchange. Associated with each is a group of common user tasks. Each task relies upon a TCP/IP link between two machines.

Messaging: (based on the Simple Mail Transfer Protocol (SMTP)) provides one-to-one e-mail communication between individuals. It also provides one-to-many communication, as when one message is sent to an explicit "distribution list," and many-to-many communication as groups "discuss" topics via electronic conferences or forums.

Remote login: (based on the Telnet and rlogin protocols) provides a virtual terminal connection between two cooperating machines. Thus users at a remote location may connect to machines with which they have an account (such as their home institution's machine or a commercial provider like Dialog or OCLC), or with public access computers such as those that run online public access library catalogs (OPACs), as well as with non-bibliographic databases.

File exchange: (based on the File Transfer Protocol (FTP)) provides a connection between two machines and allows the transfer of files between those machines. Files may be computer programs, textual documents, or digitized images and sounds. Files are often gathered in public access archives and made available to anyone with FTP capabilities on the Internet.

## An Additional Perspective: Size

### Small

People often identify networks according to geographic size or dispersal of the connected machines. Thus you may be well aware of the resources available on your local area network (LAN), such as shared software and a printer. LANs are frequently interconnected to create a campus network or metropolitan area network (MAN). As networks encompass wider areas (larger geographic distances), usually by interconnecting LANs and MANs, they receive the imprecise label of a wide area network (WAN).

### Large

The Internet is often described as a network of networks and encompasses all sizes of networks to become a truly global network (not surprisingly, no one has bothered to coin GAN - a global area network). There are two more important categories of constituent networks in the Internet: the regional networks and the NSFnet "backbone" network. The regional networks, such as BARRNet, SURANet, NYSERNet, and others are all internetworked. The links between them are most often provided by the NSFnet, called the "backbone" of the U.S.-based part of the Internet, and funded historically by the Defense department (as ARPANET), and currently by the National Science Foundation.

### Even Larger

There are other wide area networks, such as BITNET, FIDOnet, and Usenet that connect various machines around the world. With the addition of gateways between the Internet and these networks the geographic dispersion of connected machines is amazing. In most cases the gateways can only translate messages or e-mail to send from one network to another. But that still yields connectivity to countless places and people.

**Note:** Outlines of this material, suitable for training purposes, are available in section H, *Trainer's Aids*. Supplementary materials, such as network diagrams, are in Section I, the *Appendix*.

# Names and Addresses

**Introduction**

Understanding the use of names and addresses for people, machines, and resources on the Internet is critical for successful Internet use. Metaphorically it is similar to knowing how to reach the right destination on a trip, or to enter the appropriate restroom (without, necessarily, the same embarrassment if mistaken). It is as important as having a correct phone number or postal address.

Fortunately, it is no more complex than phone numbers and postal addresses. But like those forms of identifying a person, organization, or geographic location, usually via a phone, house, or post office box, Internet addresses have rules and conventions for use. The main rules involve the distinctions between a person or user, a named machine or process, a numbered Internet machine, and a physical network device.

The two main types of addresses used are textual (domain) names of machines as contrasted with Internet or IP numeric addresses. For example:

| Domain Name Address | Equivalent IP Numeric Address |
|---|---|
| melvyl.ucop.edu | 31.1.0.11 |

**Internet Protocol "IP" Numeric Addresses**

Each machine that uses TCP/IP protocols and that is "on the Internet" must be distinguished from every other machine by a unique Internet number or address. The number is made up of four numeric pieces joined by periods. Each part is represented by eight bits representing a decimal number from 0 to 255. Thus the whole IP address is actually a 32 bit number. For example, 31.1.0.11 is the IP address for the computer that runs the University of California's online catalog, "Melvyl." The pieces of the IP address are hierarchical, with the leftmost numbers representing a large network, followed by numbers representing a "subnet" and specific machine.

The IP address is always assigned by a network administrator but is based on the configuration of the networks (local, regional, and national) to which a machine belongs. Note that even with the millions of numbers available by using 32 bits in an IP address, there are already concerns about running out of unique addresses for Internet machines.

**Domain Name Addresses**

Originally, machines connected via the TCP/IP protocols were identified to each other and to users only by their IP numeric address as described above. It became obvious that the numeric addresses were clumsy for people to use and so textual equivalents were added. Therefore 31.1.0.11 is associated with "melvyl.ucop.edu," a more friendly name, particularly if you happen to know that "Melvyl" is a very large online library catalog, "ucop" stands for the University of California Office of the President, and that "edu" indicates an

**Domain Name Addresses**
*cont'd*

"educational institution" (organizational category). For the most part, names are chosen to be indicative of the name of the machine and the type of service and organization that owns or supports the service. As with numeric addresses the names are hierarchic, but, unfortunately, are organized in reverse fashion, from most specific (machine name; e.g. "melvyl") at the left, to most general *top-level* domain ( e.g., "edu") to the right. A full name, including the middle portion which indicates the sponsoring organization (such as "ucop" above, or "harvard" in "hollis.harvard.edu" – another popular library catalog), is called a *Fully Qualified Domain Name.*

Other important top-level domains include organizational domains, such as:

| | |
|---|---|
| com | Usually a commercial institution; e.g. apple.com for Apple Computer. |
| gov | A government site; e.g. nasa.gov for NASA. |
| mil | A military site; e.g. af.mil for the Air Force |
| org | A hard-to-classify site; e.g. oclc.org for OCLC |

Some top-level domains are geographic, usually based on the country, such as:

| | |
|---|---|
| au | Australia |
| ca | Canada |
| us | USA |

Each part of the name must be assigned by the proper authority. Thus, the top-level domains are "owned" and administered by the General Services Incorporated Network Information Center (GSI NIC); lower level domain names such as "ucop" or "harvard" are registered with it. Likewise, the machine names "melvyl" or "hollis" are approved by the network administration at the University of California and Harvard, respectively.

Machines must consult databases to translate domain names to IP addresses (each domain has at least two machines that provide this translating service). For most Internet services, either the domain name or the IP address will work to reach the machine. However, it is increasingly true that the domain name is preferred, both for ease of use, and because domain names remain fairly stable, while their equivalent IP addresses can and do change.

**Underneath It All – Physical Level Names**

The complexity keeps getting deeper. At the most basic level — the "physical" layer, in networking terms — there is yet another address that is needed for the machines to communicate: the local area network physical address. The IP number works independently of the type of machine or the specific type of local network that the machine is attached to, ethernet versus token-ring, for example. Nevertheless, at some point the local network will need to find a machine based upon its physical address as determined by the low level protocols, e.g. an Ethernet address. Fortunately, the conversion from IP address to physical address is taken care of invisibly by the network software. For the user, this is rarely an important issue, but it is extremely important for administrators. Knowledge of this distinction helps create network sophistication.

## Adding People

Adding the distinction of a user or "account holder" at a particular machine is fairly straightforward for Internet machines. Using the Internet name for the computer system, one simply prefaces it with the "account ID" or "user name" and the "at" symbol @. Thus, for example, you may reach the authors by addressing mail to:

jlo-lis@cmsa.berkeley.edu (for John Ober)
rtennant@library.berkeley.edu (for Roy Tennant)
alipow@library.berkeley.edu (for Anne Lipow).

Institutions vary widely in the way they form account IDs or user names. Last name preceded by a first name leading initial is fairly common, but some institutions seem to prefer numbers, or strange configurations of numbers, letters, and other characters. An underscore character "_" or a period "." is sometimes used to separate first and last names (e.g., roy_tennant or roy.tennant) in e-mail addresses.

## What's Essential

The analogy between network addresses and postal addresses or telephone numbers holds up past the immediate comparisons. Just as with postal addresses, it is difficult to communicate with a person (or organization or machine) electronically unless you know the network address. For the Internet, knowledge of either the IP number or the textual domain name will allow use of Internet services such as FTP and TELNET, while the textual name is generally easier to remember and is what you should use. Most e-mail systems seem to require the textual name of the Internet machine on which an account is located. One of the important needs being addressed in various ways is the development of name and address finding tools. There is not yet a directory service equivalent to telephone directory service or white pages, or even the postal zip code directory. Guides and directories to electronic addresses such as those listed in the bibliography and throughout this book are an important beginning. Online tools, such as the "Whois" command (see "E-Mail Tips and Tricks: Finding Addresses" in the *Electronic Mail* section) are also being developed.

# Evolution of Networks & Network Services

**Introduction**

It is nearly impossible for one person, or one document such as this, to note every evolutionary step. The oft-cited geometric growth in the computer industry occurs in the general world of networking as well. However, changes to the Internet and its use can be categorized by the technological, social/ political, and functional perspectives mentioned earlier.

**Technological changes**

As with computers in general, network technology is changing drastically in terms of speed and size. Tenfold or one hundredfold increases in capacity and speed are common between "generations" of technology, for example from T1 (1.5 megabits per second) to T3 (45 megabits per second) speeds. The amount of traffic flowing into the NSFnet backbone shows similar increases. Economies of scale and scope are not the only driving forces behind these changes. In addition to the pure drive for technological innovation there are desirable applications, such as the transfer and real-time remote manipulation of still or moving images, for which network capabilities do not yet exist. On the other hand, there are opportunities to tap the latent capabilities of the networks, for example by massively distributed processing — sharing the processing power of the micros and mainframes that are often idle while attached to the networks.

**Social/Political changes**

Issues not only of technological development, but also of the distribution of network resources and network access, have joined economic and political agendas. Historically, access to the Internet has been restricted to people affiliated with institutions of higher education and research organizations. But the pressures to expand access has increased in recent years. For example, in the United States the enabling legislation for the National Research and Education Network (NREN) addresses both higher technological perfor- mance and wider distribution of access, particularly to K-12 educators and students. A wide variety of other issues reflect a desperate struggle to keep public policy from lagging too far behind technical capability. These include:

> "Acceptable uses" of publicly funded networks
> Copyright issues of Internet accessible or delivered material
> Commercialization and privatization of the historically public-funded
> > Internet
> Protection of privacy given increased access to various data
> Equitable access to information, especially publicly produced information
> Education and retraining to create or maintain network "literacy"
> Quality control of networked information
> Integration of network and print tools and industries

In an increasingly familiar catch-22, debate about these issues often takes place on the networks themselves. The reader is encouraged to consult the resources in the bibliography and mentioned in the E-mail, Telnet, and FTP chapters to join the debates and read the materials produced by their participants. Various electronic conferences and FTP and Telnet sites are maintained by groups such as the Electronic Frontier Foundation, The Coalition for Networked Information, the Internet Society, Computer Profes- sionals for Social Responsibility, and others.

## Functional Changes — "Extended services"

It can easily be argued that the basic tools for using the Internet — electronic mail, remote login, and file transfer — are awkward to use, requiring the memorization of special sets of commands and a great deal of prior knowledge about the location of resources. There are several current attempts to improve or extend the Internet functions and services.

### Improved access

One strategy for improving access is to use one of the tools, usually Telnet, to get to a machine that has a more friendly user interface or provides a specialized service. Some of the public access Telnet sites, including several library sites and "Freenets" (see the *Fact Sheets* and *Telnet* sections) attempt to provide a friendly user interface to other network services. A variant of this strategy is to use local software that provides menu-driven access to remote systems; see, for example, LIBS and HYTELNET in the *Fact Sheets* section.

Another way to improve access is to use online guides or search services for Internet resources: using remote login (Telnet) you can get to a service which searches a database and then provides addresses or location information. The Archie service employs this strategy to help users locate files available for FTP (see *Fact Sheets*).

### Client/Server Applications

The Wide Area Information Servers project (WAIS) and Gopher software (both discussed more fully in the *Fact Sheets*), are examples of creating user friendly interface software that runs on a local machine (the client) with which you can construct various requests and initiate queries of remote machines (the servers). With this strategy users do most of their work on the local desktop machine and then instruct it to run the search, perhaps on several different servers in succession. This allows the user to spend less time as an "Internet scavenger" and also ties up fewer network resources with extended online sessions. Work is being done to extend this strategy until software "user agents" are able to roam the Internet looking for information that fits the current interests of the user. The user could receive periodic reports (for example, daily, even hourly) of new information without having to conduct the exploration directly at all.

### Virtual Realities

Much speculation and several Internet experiments are devoted to the construction of electronic arenas that more closely mimic the appearance or feel of real places or services. Thus "multi-user dimensions" allow real-time interaction between several people connected to a system at once. The interaction takes place in textually-described rooms and corridors which, for example, are like conference or meeting rooms. A user may also "enter" library reference rooms or the card catalog room, which would of course allow electronic access to a catalog.

An important goal of all of these functional extensions is to reduce — eventually in fact, eliminate — the user's need to know the location of either the machine or the information source.

# C | Important Information for Beginners

*This section contains:*

- Glossary
- Getting Connected
- Internet Service Providers
- How to Keep Current
- Bibliography

# Glossary

**Account**   When you use a particular computer system, you are given an account. Associated with the account are a unique user name and a password. You enter these to show that you are a legitimate user of the system.

**Addresses**   A unique name (or number) identifying a computer user or computer is called an address. Addresses are used in network communications in transmitting messages to a particular person or machine.

**Archie**   A database and related programs giving the user information about the contents of various archives (see Fact Sheets).

**Archive**   Collections of files related to a particular subject, which are stored on a computer and made available for distributions to the network community, usually via anonymous FTP.

**ASCII**   A standard method for encoding characters — "text" files are usually ASCII files. ASCII has codes representing upper and lower case letters, the numerals, and punctuation. ASCII is an acronym for American Standard Code for Information Interchange.

**Backbone**   A high speed connection within a network which connects shorter (usually slower) branch circuits. The NSFNet is generally considered to be the backbone network of the Internet in the U.S.

**Bandwidth**   A measure of capacity and speed of the links between computing devices. Measured in kilobits per second (Kbps), megabits per second (Mbps), or gigabits per second (Gbps).

**Binary file**   All files which are not text files are considered binary files. Any combination of bits is possible with a binary file.

**BITNET**   Cooperative education and research network, primarily provides e-mail services.

**Client**   A program running on a computer which requests services from another program, often called a "server," and usually running on a remote computer.

**Datagram**   A formatted set of electronic data used in communication between computer systems. The datagram consists of two parts: the data proper which may be part of a longer message, and the header which indicates the source, the destination, the type of data, etc.

**Directory**   Files on many computer systems are grouped together in directories. There is often a directory for each user, holding the files owned by that user, and also directories holding public files. Files common to a topic are often organized into separate directories or sub-directories.

**Directory Service**   A service on a network giving information about sites, computers, resources, or users in the area.

**Domain**   A classification category used for identifying computers in a network. The names of successive domains are used to form a unique name by which the computer is known to the network.

## Glossary cont'd

**Domain Name**  A structured name for a computer in a network, in the form melvyl.ucop.edu.  Uniqueness is ensured by having a hierarchy of naming authorities, each one responsible for approving the names in its immediate domain.

**Download/downloading**   The process of transferring files to your *local* machine using communications software and a modem. Often the last step necessary to have your "own" copy of a file.

**E-mail**  Electronic mail; online messaging services between computer users.

**E-serial**  (Or E-journal) A periodical distributed in electronic form.

**E-text**  The full-text of a document available in electronic format (often through FTP).

**EARN**  European Academic and Research Network. A European equivalent to BITNET. Uses BITNET-type protocols.

**edu**  The standard highest level domain name used to identify educational institutions.

**Finger**  A simple network service which will report if a particular user is currently logged in on a particular node on the net.

**FTP**   File Transfer Protocol, allows moving files from one computer to another.

**Gateway**   A computer which connects two networks, often converting protocols on messages from one network to the other. In particular, an Internet gateway routes IP datagrams among the networks it connects. Also used to refer in general to a system capability that provides direct access to other, remote networks or services.

**Gopher**   Client/server software providing flexible access to Internet resources developed at the University of Minnesota (see Fact Sheets).

**Host**  A computer system on which you can hold an interactive session, or which is the source of network services.

**HYTELNET**   A program that provides flexible connection to a variety of networked information resources including online public access catalogs (see Fact Sheets).

**Internet**   The international network of networks based on the TCP/IP protocol. Also, with a small "i" any interconnected set of networks.

**IP address**  A specially formulated number assigned to Internet computers, e.g., "31.1.0.11".

**JANET**  The academic and research network in the United Kingdom.  It is an acronym for Joint Academic Network.

**Knowbot**  *Knowledge robots* designed to search files on the Internet. It is a registered trademark of the Corporation for National Research Initiatives.

**Listserv (listserver)**   BITNET service (software) providing distributed messages that form conferences and allow the archiving of files and messages which can be searched and retrieved.

**Login**   An opening procedure to identify yourself to a system as a legitimate user and begin a session.   Normally, to login you need to give a valid user name and password.   The word "logon" is also used.

**Logout**   A closing procedure to formally end a session with a system. Breaking a network connection will not necessarily result in logging you out.   The word "logoff" is also used.

**Name**   A textual string which is mapped to an IP address, e.g., "melvyl.ucop.edu".

**Nameserver**   A computer in a network responsible for keeping the name and address mapping tables, and for providing that information on request (usually from other machines, not people directly).

**Node**   A single computer within a network.

**OSI**   An abbreviation for Open Systems Interconnect, an internationally agreed upon set of standards for computer connection. In some ways it "competes" with TCP/IP. It is not yet widely used, especially in the United States.

**Protocol**   Specific rules defining one part of the transmission and receipt of information across a data communications link. In sets, or suites, they govern communication between entities, including type, size, and format of data units.

**RFC**   "Request for Comments"; the documents which contain the standards and other information for the TCP/IP protocols and the Internet in general. They are available at several sites through anonymous FTP (see Fact Sheets).

**RLOGIN**   A program specific to BSD 4.3 UNIX machines that allows remote login, much like Telnet (see "Introduction to Remote Login").

**Routing**   Finding an effective or efficient path through a network to a destination computer.   Routing is almost always handled by the network or communication software.

**Server**   A program (or generically, a computer) that provides services, such as files or access to a database, when requested by a (usually remote) "client" process.

**Speed**   see bandwidth

**SMTP**   (Simple Mail Transfer Protocol) - the Internet standard protocol for transferring electronic mail messages.

**T1, T3**   Standards that represent 1.544 megabits (T1) and 45 megabits (T3) per second transmission speeds in data communications.

**TCP/IP**   (Transmission Control Protocol/Internet Protocol) - common designation for the Internet suite of protocols.

**Telnet**   Internet protocol providing connection ("remote login") to a remote computer. Also, generally the name of the program implementing the protocol.

**tn3270**   A version of the Telnet software which allows connection to IBM mainframes by emulating a popular IBM terminal, the "3270" terminal.

**UNIX**   An operating system available for a wide range of computers. Originally developed at AT&T Bell Labs. Ultrix and Solaris are among its descendants.

**Usenet**   A worldwide Unix-based network that supports the distribution of messages (see Usenet News Fact Sheet).

**Username or ID**   Address representing a personal account on a large computer, e.g., "jlo-lis@cmsa.berkeley.edu"

**UUCP**   Unix to Unix Copy Program. A networking protocol with less functionality than TCP/IP used by Usenet.

**VMS**   The operating system used by Digital Equipment Corporation's VAX Computers. Both "VAX" and "VMS" are registered trademarks.

**VT100**   A standard terminal type, supported by many computer systems, and emulated by many terminals or personal computers which are not themselves VT100 terminals.

**X.25**   A data communications protocol developed to govern how data passes into and out of public data communications networks such as Telenet and Tymnet.

**WAIS**   Wide Area Information Servers; Client/Server software providing searching and retrieval of various databases. Based on Z39.50 protocols and developed by Thinking Machines, Inc. (see Fact Sheets).

**Z39.50**   A U.S. based protocol (with international, OSI, counterparts) that provides for the exchange of information, such as full text or catalog records, between dissimilar computer systems.

# Getting Connected

**Introduction**

There are several ways to gain access to the Internet:
- Dialup methods (using a personal computer and a modem)

    *Dialup to an Internet host using standard communications software*

    For some users, the cheapest and easiest way to get an Internet connection is to dialup an Internet-connected computer via their PC with communications software and a modem. But first you must obtain an account on that Internet-connected computer.

    *Dialup to an Internet host computer using SLIP (Serial Line Internet Protocol — see Fact Sheets)*

    A way to obtain many of the benefits of direct connection to the Internet without a dedicated line is to use SLIP. For example, SLIP allows you to transfer files via FTP directly to your personal computer, rather than being required to go through an intermediary step as you would with a simple dialup connection.

- Direct connection (requires a dedicated line to your computer or LAN)

    Many academic institutions and some private companies are well-networked and users in these locations may find it relatively easy, as well as better functionally, to obtain a direct connection.

Investigate several options to compare price, functionality, ease of use, and support. You are likely to need some sort of assistance and you would be well advised to have a means in place to obtain that assistance. Below are several strategies that you can consider for obtaining your Internet connection; which one will work best for you depends upon your particular situation.

**Your Institution**

If you work for a large company or a college or university, ask around to see if your institution is already connected to the Internet. If it is, then investigate the possibility of connecting your PC or workstation directly to the network. If you cannot or do not wish to connect directly, try to obtain an account on a computer running the UNIX operating system. UNIX has a number of functions that make it a particularly good operating system for networking.

**Colleges or Universities**

Contact your local college or university to see if they are connected to the Internet and if they rent computer accounts to off-campus users. Many will do so. In general, the larger the institution is, the more likely it is connected to the Internet.

**Regional Networks**

Check with your regional networking organization to see if they offer low-cost Internet access services. Your local college or university computing center staff will know what organization this is and how to contact it. A list of these organizations is on the following pages.

**Network Service Resellers**

Look for network service resellers. These are private companies that obtain network services from network service providers (such as regional networking organizations) and resell service to individual users. See the following pages for examples of those companies. They may be listed under various subjects in the yellow pages of your phone book. They often will cater to low-budget users by offering dialup services as well as direct-connect service.

# Internet Service Providers

## Introduction

The following is a list of organizations that provide Internet service. This list is not comprehensive and mention here does not imply endorsement. Some of these organizations do not offer services to individual users; contact the organization to find out what services are offered.

## United States

| NETWORK | SERVICE AREA | CONTACT | PHONE |
|---|---|---|---|
| Alternet | US and Int'l | UUNET | (800) 4UUNET3 |
| ANS | US and Int'l | Joel Maloff | (313) 663-7610 |
| BARRNET | Bay Area, CA | Paul Baer | (415) 723-7520 |
| CERFnet | West. US & Int'l | CERFnet Hotline | (800) 876-2373 |
| CICnet | (MN, WI, IA, IN, IL, MI, OH) | John Hankins | (313) 998-6102 |
| CO Supernet | Colorado | Ken Harmon | (303) 273-3475 |
| CONCERT | North Carolina | Joe Ragland | (919) 248-1404 |
| Int'l Connections Manager (ICM) | International | Robert Collet | (703) 904-2230 |
| INet | Indiana (IN) | Dick Ellis | (812) 855-4240 |
| JVNCnet | US and Int'l | Sergio Heker | (800) 35TIGER |
| Los Nettos | Los Angeles (CA) | Ann W. Cooper | (310) 822-1511 |
| MichNet/Merit | Michigan (MI) | Jeff Ogden | (313) 764-9430 |
| MIDnet | (NE, OK, AR, MO, IA, KS, SD) | Dale Finkelson | (402) 472-5032 |
| MRnet | Minnesota (MN) | Dennis Fazio | (612) 342-2570 |
| MSEN | Michigan (MI) | Owen Medd | (313) 741-1120 |
| NEARnet | (ME, NH, VT, CT, RI, MA) | John Curran | (617) 873-8730 |
| netILLINOIS | Illinois (IL) | Joel L. Hartman | (309) 677-3100 |
| NevadaNet | Nevada (NV) | Don Zitter | (702) 784-6133 |
| NorthwestNet | (WA, OR, ID, MT, ND, WY, AK) | Eric Hood | (206) 562-3000 |
| NYSERnet | New York (NY) | Jim Luckett | (315) 443-4120 |
| OARnet | Ohio (OH) | Alison Brown | (614) 292-8100 |
| PACCOM | Hawaii (HI) & Int'l | Torben Nielsen | (808) 956-3499 |
| PREPnet | Pennsylvania (PA) | Thomas Bajzek | (412) 268-7870 |
| PSCNET | (PA, OH, WV) | Eugene Hastings | (412) 268-4960 |
| PSINet | US and Int'l | PSI, Inc. | (800) 82PSI82 |
| SDSCnet | San Diego (CA) | Paul Love | (619) 534-5043 |
| Sesquinet | Texas (TX) | Farrell Gerbode | (713) 527-4988 |
| SprintLink | US and Int'l | Bob Doyle | (703) 904-2230 |
| SURAnet | Southeastern US | Jack Hahn | (301) 982-4600 |
| THEnet | Texas (TX) | Tracy L. Parker | (512) 471-2444 |
| VERnet | Virginia (VA) | James Jokl | (804) 924-0616 |
| Westnet | (AZ, CO, ID, NM, UT, WY) | Pat Burns | (303) 491-7260 |
| WiscNet | Wisconsin (WI) | Tad Pinkerton | (608) 262-8874 |
| WVNET | West Virginia (WV) | Harper Grimm | (304) 293-5192 |

**Canada**

| NETWORK | SERVICE AREA | CONTACT | PHONE |
|---------|--------------|---------|-------|
| ARnet | Alberta | Walter Neilson | (403) 450-5188 |
| BCnet | British Columbia | Mike Patterson | (604) 822-3932 |
| MBnet | Manitoba | Gerry Miller | (204) 474-8230 |
| AccessNB | New Brunswick | David MacNeil | (506) 453-4573 |
| NLnet | Newfoundland and Labrador | Wilf Bussey | (709) 737-8329 |
| NSTN | Nova Scotia | Michael Martineau | (902) 468-NSTN |
| ONet | Ontario | Andy Bjerring | (519) 661-2151 |
| PEINet | Prince Edward Island | Jim Hancock | (902) 566-0450 |
| RISQ | Quebec | Bernard Turcotte | (514) 340-5700 |
| SASK#net | Saskatchewan | Dean C. Jones | (306) 966-4860 |

**Worldwide**

For information on network service providers around the world, see the NSF Network Service Center's *Network Provider Referral List*, which is available for anonymous FTP from host nnsc.nsf.net, in directory nsfnet, filename referral-list (see the section "Internet File Transfer" in this book for information on using FTP to retrieve files).

**Network Service Resellers**

Below are representative samples of the kinds of organizations you may find in your area. Also, there are many other networking organizations (primarily commercial networks) that provide e-mail connectivity to the Internet, but do not support Telnet or FTP access.

**CAPCON** A regional library Network in the Washington, DC area reselling SURAnet services. Call (202) 331-5771 for information.

**CLASS** A regional library Network in California reselling CERFNet services. Call (800) 488-4559 for more information.

**Colleges and Universities** Colleges and universities will sometimes allow persons unaffiliated with the campus to rent an account on a campus computer that is connected to the Internet.

**NETCOM** A private company in the San Francsico Bay Area that rents low-cost UNIX accounts on an Internet-connected computer. Call (408) 554-UNIX for more information.

**Note:** Most of this information is provided courtesy of the National Science Foundation Network Service Center; accurate as of July 2, 1992. The NSF Network Service Center's *Network Provider Referral List*, is available for anonymous FTP from host nnsc.nsf.net, in directory nsfnet, filename referral-list.

# How to Keep Current

**Two steps forward, one back**

Keeping up with the "net" is difficult if not outright impossible. The reason for this is that the Internet is so large, diverse, and ever-changing. Some of what you know today will not be true tomorrow. And understanding the totality of information resources on the Internet is nearly as difficult as understanding the totality of published reference sources currently in print. So realize that you cannot know all that you would *like* to know about the Internet and be content with what you can find out with a reasonable amount of effort. Also, more tools are now available to help you locate and use Internet information resources and it is likely that this trend toward user-utility, if not user-friendliness, will continue.

**Cultivate network contacts**

One of the best ways to keep current, which can also be professionally rewarding and just plain fun, is to become friends with others on the network. In networking, as in real life, it is impossible to keep up with everything you're interested in on your own. Others on the network who know your interests can inform you of things you might have missed. And you will most likely return the favor. To start a net friendship often all that is needed is for you to strike up an electronic conversation with someone. If you noticed that someone who posts to an electronic discussion has interesting and informative things to say, write them and tell them so. Tell them something that you think may interest them. You may be surprised how easy and yet how rewarding it can be.

**Conferences and workshops**

Conference programs and workshops can be an excellent way to keep informed. Information presented at these sessions is likely to be very current, unlike many print sources. Take note of any print or network information resources that are named; they are likely to be the essential references or the best examples of particular types of Internet resources.

**Electronic discussions**

One of the best ways to keep up with new developments in networked information resources is to subscribe to one or more electronic discussions. The currency of the information on these lists as well as the chance for serendipitous discovery make them a good resource for staying current. These discussions can also help you to identify like-minded individuals with whom you can directly correspond (see "Cultivate network contacts" above). A few of the more important electronic discussions for networked information resource discovery are outlined below. For additional discussion lists, see "Electronic Discussions for Librarians" in the Electronic Mail section.

*CWIS-L*
The Campus-Wide Information Systems discussion list posts notices of new college and university information systems available for Internet access, as does Judy Hallman's directory of CWISs. To subscribe, send the message "SUB CWIS-L Your Name" to LISTSERV@WUVMD.BITNET.

**Electronic discussions** *cont'd*

*LIB_HYTELNET*
This list posts information on new information resources on the Internet before they are made more widely available in a new release of HYTELNET, the hypertext guide/gateway to Internet resources produced by Peter Scott of the University of Saskatchewan. Send e-mail to Peter Scott requesting to be added to the list: scott@sklib.usask.ca.

*PACS-L*
The Public Access Computer Systems Forum is the premier library discussion list. It is closely moderated (several postings are often grouped into one message based upon topic, and spurious messages are trapped before they are posted to the list), and therefore tends to be more rewarding than other, unmoderated lists. To subscribe, send the message "SUB PACS-L Your Name" to LISTSERV@UHUPVM1.BITNET. From time to time Charle Bailey, Jr. posts a list of library-related discussions on PACS-L.

*resource-guide-request@nnsc.nsf.net*
This is the distribution list for the *Internet Resource Guide* distributed by the National Science Foundation Network Service Center. As new resources are added to the *Guide*, you will either be sent the update or notified of how to obtain it, depending on which list (receive updates in text format, PostScript® format, or where to get it via FTP) to which you ask to subscribe. Send a free-text request to the address above to subscribe.

**Periodicals**

A few selected journals and newsletters are listed below which may be useful to you for keeping current in computer networking. This list is by no means comprehensive; these days you can find pertinent information in a wide variety of publications.

*Current Cites*
A monthly current awareness newsletter of annotated citations from library and computer literature. It is posted on PACS-L (see above) and PACS-P (publications only), is available as a Gopher and WAIS source, and can be obtained via FTP from ftp.cni.org. The most recent six issues can also be read online via the MELVYL catalog (TELNET to melvyl.ucop.edu, enter "show current cites" when connected). Direct e-mail subscriptions are available by contacting the editor, David Robison, at drobison@library.berkeley.edu.

*DATABASE*
A journal published by ONLINE, Inc. (800) 248-8466.

*EDUCOM Review*
The journal of EDUCOM, the academic computing organization that administers BITNET. EDUCOM is also a partner in the Coalition for Networked Information and the *EDUCOM Review* has been a treasure trove of networking articles for years. Contact PUBS@EDUCOM.EDU or (202) 872-4200 for subscription information.

*EFFector Online*
The electronic journal of the Electronic Frontier Foundation, founded by Mitch Kapor of Lotus 1-2-3 fame. For more information on EFF, see the section on organizations below. Send subscription request to eff@eff.org.

*Electronic Networking: Research, Applications and Policy*
A quarterly journal from Meckler (800) 635-5537 on many different aspects of computer networking.

*Information Technology and Libraries*
The quarterly journal of the Library and Information Technology Association of ALA. Members of the association receive it automatically; non-member subscriptions are available. Contact the American Library Association at (312) 944-6780 for more information.

*Internet Monthly Report*
An electronic publication on mostly technical aspects of the Internet; nonetheless some nuggets of more widely useful information can be found here. To subscribe, send an e-mail message to: imr-request@isi.edu.

*Internet Society News*
Published quarterly by the Internet Society. Contact the society at (703) 620-8990 or isoc@nri.reston.va.us for more information.

*Library Hi Tech*
This journal has often featured articles on networking and has even been known to devote an entire issue to the topic. Published by Pierian Press (800) 678-2435.

*Matrix News*
A monthly newsletter published by John Quarterman of *Matrix* fame (see bibliography). Available from Matrix Information and Directory Services, 701 Brazos, Suite 500, Austin, TX 78701-3243.

*NetMonth*
An electronic netjournal that has appeared quite erratically lately. Send the message "SUB NETMONTH Your Name" to LISTSERV@MARIST.BITNET.

*ONLINE*
A monthly journal from Online, Inc., the same folks who bring you *DATABASE* (800) 248-8466.

*Public Access Computer Systems Review*
An electronic journal that grew out of the electronic discussion PACS-L. The table of contents and access instructions are posted to PACS-L, and its companion list of publications-only, PACS-P. Send the message "SUB PACS-P Your Name" to LISTSERV@UHUPVM1.BITNET to receive this and other publications only.

*Research and Education Networking*
A monthly newsletter-type publication from Meckler, (800) 635-5537.

## Organizations

*Coalition for Networked Information*
Formed by the Association of Research Libraries, CAUSE, and EDUCOM (two higher education computing organizations), CNI is working to make Internet information resources more accessible, to increase knowledge about networked resources, and to enhance and increase these resources. Based in Washington, DC, the organization accomplishes work through various "Working Groups" that are chaired or co-chaired by parties active in particular areas of networking. For more information, take a look at the files available at ftp.cni.org for anonymous FTP or contact:

Joan Lippincott
Assistant Director
Coalition for Networked Information
1527 New Hampshire, NW
Washington, DC 20036

(202) 232-2466
(202) 462-7849 Fax
joan@cni.org

*Electronic Frontier Foundation*
Founded and led by Mitch Kapor of Lotus 1-2-3 fame, EFF strives to protect civil liberties for the network community, to support educational activities relating to networking, to develop an awareness among policy makers regarding networking issues, and to encourage and support the development of new tools to help network users. For more information, take a look at the files available at ftp.eff.org for anonymous FTP or contact:

Electronic Frontier Foundation
155 Second Street, #1
Cambridge, MA 02141
(617) 864-0665
(617) 864-0866 Fax
eff@eff.org

*The Internet Society*
Created by the Corporation for National Research Initiatives (CNRI), EDUCOM, and the Internet Activities Board, the Internet Society plans to provide assistance and support to groups and organizations interested in the use, operation, and evolution of the Internet. At the first annual meeting of the society (the INET Conference in Kobe, Japan) in June 1992, the Internet Activities Board (IAB) and its activities (Internet Engineering Task Force, Internet Research Task Force) were merged into the Internet Society (ISOC) For more information, contact:

The Internet Society
1895 Preston White Drive, Suite 100
Reston, VA 22091
(703) 620-8990
(703) 620-0913
isoc@nri.reston.va.us

# Bibliography

**Introduction**

The literature about the Internet and the resources available on it has expanded dramatically in the last two years, particularly in the library profession. Whereas most of the literature even just a couple of years ago was technical in nature or directed to computing professionals, now there are many more articles, books, and electronic documents written expressly for Internet novices than it would be possible for us to cover here. We have tried to identify a select number of essential references while hoping that our readers realize that much more exists that can be helpful as well. Deidre Stanton's excellent bibliography can point you to a number of other sources we did not cover here. Also, additional citations are listed in other sections of this book.

**Bibliography**

Stanton, Deidre E. *Using Networked Information Resources: A Bibliography*. Perth, WA: Author, 1992. [Available by anonymous FTP from host infolib.murdoch.edu.au, directory pub/bib, filename stanton.bib or stanton.bib.wp]

An extremely thorough and useful bibliography on networked information resources, both print and electronic. Access instructions are included for electronic resources. Updated periodically.

**Directories**

Barron, Billy. *UNT's Accessing On-Line Bibliographic Databases*. Denton, TX: University of North Texas, 1991. [Available by anonymous FTP from host ftp.unt.edu., directory library, filenames libraries.ps, libraries.txt, libraries.con, libraries.adr, libraries.wp]

A thorough and well-organized directory to library catalogs around the world that are accessible over the Internet. Organized by name of institution, each entry provides logon instructions and, if appropriate, referral to an appendix where basic searching instructions for most types of library catalog software can be found. Separate lists of the numeric IP addresses and contact persons for each entry provide for the type of quick-referral information that help make this directory more useful than similar documents. Highly recommended. Updated periodically.

*Interest Groups*. Menlo Park, CA: SRI International, Network Information Systems Center, 1992. [Available by anonymous FTP from host ftp.nisc.sri.com, directory netinfo, filename interest-groups]

The full list of Internet and BITNET electronic discussions. Truly a massive document.

LaQuey, Tracy L. *User's Directory of Computer Networks*. Bedford, MA: Digital Press, 1990.

See the annotation for Quarterman, John.

National Science Foundation Network Service Center. *Internet Resource Guide*. Cambridge, MA: NSF Network Service Center, 1989. [Available by anonymous FTP from host nnsc.nsf.net, directory resource-guide]

The "official" directory of Internet resources. Very incomplete, particularly regarding library catalogs and campus-wide information systems. Updated periodically.

## Directories
### cont'd

Quarterman, John S. *The Matrix: Computer Networks and Conferencing Systems Worldwide*. Bedford, MA: Digital Press, 1990.

The acknowledged essential reference guide to computer networks. This one, along with Tracy LaQuey's book are still the only game in town for describing the infrastructure of the Internet and its constituent networks. These are not guides for using the net, but rather are for trying to make sense of which networks exist and how they tie together.

St. George, Art and Ron Larsen. *Internet-Accessible Library Catalogs and Databases*. Albuquerque, NM:University of New Mexico, 1991. [Available by anonymous FTP from host ariel.unm.edu, directory library, filename internet.library]

A thorough directory of library catalogs on the Internet. Organized geographically. Updated periodically.

Strangelove, Michael and Diane Kovacs. *Directory of Electronic Journals, Newsletters and Academic Discussion Lists*. Washington, DC: Association of Research Libraries, 1992.[The electronic journals portion is available by sending the message GET EJOURNL1 DIRECTRY and GET EJOURNL2 DIRECTRY to listserv@acadvm1.uottawa.ca; the academic discussion lists portion is available by sending the messages GET ACADLIST FILE1, GET ACADLIST FILE2 ...GET ACADLIST FILE7 to LISTSERV@KENTVM.BITNET]

Organized into two parts: 1) Journals and Newsletters (by Michael Strangelove, and 2) Academic Discussion Lists and Interest Groups (by Diane Kovacs), this guide is an essential directory to these resources. The subject categorization of academic discussion lists is particularly helpful, as these are often difficult to locate by any other means. Updated periodically.

## General Information

"Communications, Computers and Networks." *Scientific American* [Special issue]. 265(3) (September 1991).

This entire issue is devoted to computer networks, and is comprised of articles from some of the heavy hitters of the networking world. An interesting and wide-ranging introduction.

*High Performance Computing Act of 1991*. Passed by the U.S. Congress, and signed into law by President Bush on December 9, 1991.

The public law that enables development of the National Research and Education Network, which will become the backbone of the United States portion of the Internet.

LaQuey, Tracy, with Jeanne C. Ryer.*The Internet Companion: A Beginner's Guide to Global Networking*. Reading, MA: Addison-Wesley, 1993.

This is the book to hand someone who is curious what all this Internet "fuss" is about This is a great place to start in learning about the Internet and what it offers. Don't come here for detailed explanations on how to use Internet applications, but *do* come here to get the big picture and have fun while you're doing it!

**General Information cont'd**

Lynch, Clifford & Cecilia Preston "Internet Access to Information Resources." *Annual Review of Information Science and Technology.* (1990) 26:263-312.

A survey article that ranges from Memex to NREN with plenty of stops in between. Includes a massive bibliography.

Malamud, Carl. *Stacks: Interoperability in Today's Computer Networks.* Englewood Cliffs, NJ: Prentice-Hall, 1992.

A concise discussion of networks, network protocols and standards, and related issues. If the acronyms and diagrams don't scare you off, you will find that it is a very understandable explanation of some very technical topics.

Malkin, Gary Scott and April N. Marine. *FYI on Questions and Answers: Answers to Commonly asked "New Internet User" Questions.* Network Working Group, Request for Comments 1325, May 1992. [Available by anonymous FTP from host ftp.nisc.sri.com, directory /rfc, filename rfc1325.txt]

A good introduction for new users. If you're not yet familiar with anonymous FTP, ask an experienced Internet user to retrieve it for you.

McClure, Charles R., Ann P. Bishop, Philip Doty, and Howard Rosenbaum, eds. *The National Research and Education Network (NREN): Research and Policy Perspectives.* Norwood, NJ: Ablex, 1991.

One of the only resources that covers research and policy issues.

Polly, Jean Armour, "Surfing the Internet: An Introduction," *Wilson Library Bulletin,* 66(10) (June 1992): 38-42+.

An excellent beginner's overview to key Internet resources.

**Guides**

Farley, Laine, ed. *Library Resources on the Internet: Strategies for Selection and Use.* Chicago, IL: Reference and Adult Services Section, American Library Association, 1991.[Available by anonymous FTP from host dla.ucop.edu, directory pub/internet, filename libcat-guide]

The essential user's guide to Internet-accessible library catalogs. Covers basic Internet background information, directories of library catalogs, reasons for searching library catalogs via the Internet, sources for selecting appropriate catalogs to search, gateways and clients, survival tips for technical problems, searching strategies, command sets for most vendor systems, a glossary and bibliographies.

Henry, Marcia Klinger. *Search Sheets for OPACs on the Internet: A Selective Guide to U.S. OPACs Utilizing VT100 Emulation.* Westport, CT: Meckler, 1991.

The title says it all. Spotty coverage, but may grow in subsequent editions.

*Internet: Getting Started.* Edited by April Marine. Menlo Park, CA: SRI International, 1992.

Nicely formatted, with clear headings and succinct paragraphs. Useful lists, such as "Providers of dialup services"; and a comprehensive chapter on "Non-U.S. Sites."

Kehoe, Brendan P. *Zen and the Art of the Internet: A Beginner's Guide to the Internet.* 2nd edition. Englewood Cliffs, NJ: Prentice-Hall, 1993. [The 1st edition is available by anonymous ftp from host ftp.cs.widener.edu, directory pub/zen, filename zen-1.0.PS (PostScript version)]

Simple explanations of electronic mail, remote login, file transfer, and Usenet news are accompanied by brief discussions of Internet "lore" and highlighted resources.

Krol, Edward. *The Whole Internet:User's Guide and Catalog.* Sebastopol, CA: O'Reilly & Associates, 1992.

A thorough guide to using the Internet from the author of the *Hitchiker's Guide to the Internet.* Includes a sampler of Internet resources organized by subject area.

**Instruction**

McLaughlin, Pamela W., *et. al. Beyond the Walls: The World of Networked Information: An Instructional Workshop Package.* Syracuse, NY: Syracuse University, 1991.

This package both documents a particular Internet workshop/seminar held at Syracuse University in 1991, and also serves to give advice and assistance to others who wish to plan similar endeavors. The package includes a videotape scenario of a professor "B.T. Walls" using the Internet to locate information. Although the videotape is slow moving and is already becoming out-of-date, this package is one of the few examples of a workshop of this kind and may be helpful in planning such an activity.

Tennant, Roy. "Internet Basic Training: Teaching Networking Skills in Higher Education," *Electronic Networking: Research, Applications and Policy.* 1(2) (Winter 1991): 37-46.

# Notes

# D | Electronic Mail

*This section contains:*

- Introduction to Electronic Mail
- E-Mail Tips & Tricks:
  Do's & Don'ts
- E-Mail Tips & Tricks:
  Finding Addresses
- Electronic Discussions for
  Librarians
- LISTSERV Command Summary
- E-Mail Tips & Tricks:
  Electronic Discussions
- Electronic Journals
- Exercises

# Introduction to Electronic Mail

**Introduction**

Electronic mail is quickly becoming a vital communications medium for librarians. It is perhaps the most popular application of the Internet because it extends and enhances our ability to communicate with others. Through the broad communication opportunities that electronic mail and its various applications offer you, you can easily develop professional contacts with colleagues around the world that previously would have been difficult or impossible. Through electronic mail, we can now more easily overcome the barriers of geography to form professional partnerships based upon common interests. In addition, by using various e-mail services that bring together network users of common interest, it is possible to broadcast questions, discussion topics, opinions, and documents to thousands of colleagues around the world virtually simultaneously. Such power does not come without its problems, however, and judgment, restraint, and thoughtfulness are especially important when communicating electronically.

The TCP/IP protocols that define how computers connected to the Internet will communicate with each other only defines e-mail at the level of message interchange between host computers. There are no standards for e-mail software – the program that a network user would use to read and send e-mail. Therefore, network users must refer to their software documentation or computer support staff regarding the use of their electronic mail software.

Electronic mail reaches far beyond the Internet (defined as those networks supporting the TCP/IP suite of protocols). Electronic mail is exchanged with a wide variety of public and commercial networks. This connectivity comes at a price of added complexity, as the addresses required to get a message to its destination can be complex and nonintuitive.

The medium of electronic mail can be used to accomplish a number of communication tasks. Some of these are discussed in more detail below, as well as elsewhere in this section.

**Direct Communication**

What appears at first glance to be merely an electronic way to send a memo, is in fact an entirely different way to communicate, with its own benefits and shortcomings. The formatting conventions of the various forms of paper communication need not be transferred to this new medium. Electronic mail messages are composed irrespective of equal margins on left and right, your electronic return address is embedded automatically in the message, and if you assign a subject to your missive it is also included in the very top of the message automatically. This leaves you to concentrate on the *content* of the message rather than the *form*.

Electronic mail encourages informal communication. The relative ease of quickly typing a reply to a message and zapping it off, all within minutes of receiving the message that prompted it, is a powerful and efficient way to

## Direct Communication
*cont'd*

communicate. Correspondents quickly slip into frequent correspondence using quickly composed informal notes and comments rather than waiting until a fully formatted hardcopy letter can be justified. However, such ease and informality has its pitfalls. For more information on how to avoid these, refer to "E-Mail Tips & Tricks: E-Mail Do's and Don'ts" in this section.

## Electronic Discussions

There are several ways that network users with common interests can come together electronically and share questions, ideas, and opinions with one another. These discussions can be interesting, informative, and provocative. They can also be time-consuming, dull, infuriating and even useless. Whether a discussion is a waste of time or the best thing since the barcode usually depends upon how the discussion itself is organized, the participants and their contributions, and the needs and desires of the individual subscriber. For more information on this method of communication, see "Electronic Discussions for Librarians" and "E-Mail Tips & Tricks: Electronic Discussions" in this section.

## Document Distribution

Just as one can send a message via electronic mail, so can one send a file. Such a file could be a report, an article, or an entire electronic journal. Since electronic mail is passed back and forth between the Internet and numerous other networks (while use of the file transfer protocol or FTP is limited to the Internet) e-mail is the primary means of electronic journal distribution. For more information on electronic journals, see "Electronic Journals" in this section.

## Multimedia Mail

Multimedia mail is fast becoming a reality. This is the capability to send more than plain text as a mail message. A message could be comprised of a sound, an image, even a digitized video clip. Draft Internet protocol documents such as RFC1341 "MIME (Multipurpose Internet Mail Extensions): Mechanisms for Specifying and Describing the Format of Internet Message Bodies," by N. Borenstein and N. Freed, (June 1992), may help make multimedia mail a reality (for more information on RFCs, see the *Fact Sheet* "Requests for Comments").

# E-Mail Tips & Tricks: Do's & Don'ts

## Think before you send

The ease and informality of electronic mail can lull you into complacency regarding what you say and how you say it. The discipline of composition exercised in similar methods of communication (letters, memos, etc.) is often lacking in e-mail messages, sometimes to the decided detriment of both the sender and the recipient. Do not be fooled by the ease of firing off a message electronically – that message still represents you to your recipient and it should represent you well. Also, since it is so easy to forward messages to additional recipients, the intended destination of your message may not be its final resting place. The recipient of your message may forward it to someone else, who could forward it on to another person, etc. Since it is so difficult to know where your message may eventually end up, it is best to either know and trust your recipient to do you right or be judicious in what you say (see "Think thrice before you forward" below). A good rule of thumb is: write your messages as if they would appear on the front page of the *New York Times*.

## Think twice before you reply

If original messages are easy to send, replies are so easy to send they almost require no thought whatsoever. Most e-mail software will, with a one-letter "reply" command, reverse the direction of the message and await the text you enter in response. A few lines from you and another command and it is gone, speeding its way back from whence it came. Be careful of flippant, annoyed, sarcastic, or insulting replies. What is too easily sent cannot be taken back. Also, you should be aware of to whom, exactly, you are replying. Often there is one command that will reply to the sender of the message only, and another command that will reply to the sender as well as everyone who received a "carbon copy".

## Think thrice before you forward

Forwarding messages you have received to additional recipients is technically trivial and yet fraught with interpersonal peril. The rule is: before forwarding someone's message to another recipient get the permission of the original author *first*. Once forwarded, you no longer have control over that message and where it eventually ends up may prove to be embarrassing to both you and the author. Electronic friendships can be damaged, if not destroyed, by thoughtlessly forwarding a message in a way that proves harmful.

## Think overnight before you flame

There are only two kinds of electronic mail users: those who have "flamed" and those who have had the urge to flame. "Flaming" is an electronic mail term for getting up on your soapbox and ranting about something. In some cases, an e-mail correspondent will explicity define a section of message as a flame by putting "Flame on" above the passage and "Flame off" below. Although this appears to be a tried and true electronic custom, one should beware. Flaming has a strange way of singeing those who use it. Therefore, if you have the urge to flame on a topic *never* do so the day it occurs to you. Give it some time and see if you still feel so strongly. If you do flame, it is best to label it as such.

**Humor without clues is often misunderstood**

When communicating in person, we often use subtle humor to effectively make a point or to enliven a conversation. The natural tendency to do as much electronically, however, can seriously backfire if you do not provide the clues that are normally used in person that you are kidding. How does one wink or crack a sly smile electronically? Interestingly enough, there is a way. Electronic correspondents have created a panoply of crude faces using keyboard characters that can signify the use of humor or other emotions in electronic messages. Sideways smiley faces (e.g., : - ) ) are the most typical, with even a variation if you wear glasses: 8 - ). A wink can be crudely signified as well: ; - ). The point is to be explicit when you use humor. Do not leave the recipient of your message guessing about whether you are kidding or if you really do think he's an idiot. To receive a more complete list of these keyboard "pictures," send the message "GET SMILIE FACES" to LISTSERV@TEMPLEVM.BITNET.

**For more information**

Goode, Joanne and Maggie Johnson, "Putting Out the Flames: The Etiquette and Law of E-Mail," *ONLINE* 13(6) (November 1991): 61-65.

Shapiro, Norman Z. and Robert H. Anderson. *Toward an Ethics and Etiquette for Electronic Mail.* Santa Monica, CA: RAND Corporation, July 1985. [ERIC document number ED269003]

# E-Mail Tips & Tricks: Finding Addresses

**Introduction**

It is not yet possible to query one central location to discover the electronic mail address of all potential Internet correspondents. This lack of a central "white pages" facility requires e-mail users to try a number of different techniques to locate this information. Below is a list of some techniques that you may find useful, ranked in order in which you are most likely to have success. Please note that Internet resources and services change rapidly, and what is true today may not be true tomorrow. See the section "How to Keep Current" for tips on keeping your ear to the ground.

**Ask the person for his/her address**

Curiously, many network users shun the most direct, most successful method of obtaining someone's e-mail address for a variety of harder, less likely to succeed electronic techniques. Pick up the phone. Give your potential electronic correspondent a call. Most network users are delighted to give out his/her e-mail address. Telephone and address information for colleagues is usually much easier to find than e-mail addresses (e.g., the American Library Association membership directory can put you in touch with 50,000 colleagues).

**Search the subscriber list of an electronic discussion**

Electronic discussions such as the Public Access Computer Systems Forum (PACS-L) have subscriber lists that can be retrieved from the LISTSERV that maintains the mailing list. These subscriber lists consist of a one line entry per subscriber that includes their electronic mail address and their full name. For example a line out of such a file would look like this:

      rtennant@library.berkeley.edu         Roy Tennant

Such a list can thus be searched by a person's name, and their e-mail address will be found on the same line. If you have an account on a UNIX machine, find out about the "grep" command. Computers with other operating systems often have their own search command. Most word processing programs have this capability as well. For a description of how to retrieve a subscriber list of a LISTSERV discussion, see the excercise for all levels at the end of this section.

**Use the UNIX "finger" command**

The UNIX "finger" command can be used between computers running the UNIX operating system to identify persons by their name or login ID, as well as a few other bits of information. The format of the command is:

```
finger  <name or login>@<domain name>
```

For example:

```
finger tennant@library.berkeley.edu
```

If you get a message like "connection refused" or some other error message, it is possible that the computer you are trying to "finger" is not running UNIX. Some university campuses use the finger command as a directory service instead of a direct machine query. That is, a finger command sent to a campus node would return the appropriate information without needing to specify a particular computer in the domain name (e.g., "`finger joe@sonoma.edu`" rather than "`finger joe@enology.sonoma.edu`").

## Query a directory service

There are several directory services that help network users find information about other network users. Unfortunately, these services are still far from comprehensive in their coverage. A prime example of such directory services is the WHOIS service (Telnet to NIC.DDN. MIL). In addition to services that you connect to directly and search, there are also other services that will query multiple directory databases for you. An example of this technique is the Knowbot service (Telnet to nri.reston.va.us 185). The Knowbot service will query several different directory services (including the WHOIS service) and return all relevant answers to your query. Another interesting directory service is the NETFIND server at the University of Colorado (Telnet to bruno.cs.colorado.edu and login as "netfind").

# Electronic Discussions for Librarians

**Introduction**

An electronic discussion is a group of network users who have come together to discuss a particular topic. There are several methods that network users can use to participate in electronic discussions, but the basic purpose is to bring together persons of like interests to share ideas, opinions, problems and solutions. Generally they get started because someone decides to offer a discussion on a particular topic, then finds a networked computer that can "host" the discussion, and puts out an announcement that the discussion exists. Interested network users can then "subscribe" to the discussion. From then on, any message sent to the discussion is automatically distributed as electronic mail to all subscribers. This method describes LISTSERV lists and mail reflectors. Another method to participate in electronic discussions is via Usenet News (see below for a brief description).

Electronic discussions can be "moderated" or "unmoderated". The distinction denotes whether messages are automatically forwarded to all subscribers (unmoderated) or whether messages are first screened and perhaps combined with other similar messages by a human being before being sent to subscribers (moderated). All other things being equal, moderated lists are by far more useful than unmoderated ones. When messages are automatically forwarded it is possible for subscribers to receive a lot of spurious messages (for example, replies mistakenly directed at the list rather than an individual, botched subscription or unsubscription messages, etc.).

Electronic discussions can also be "open" or "closed". Anyone can subscribe to an open discussion, whereas a closed discussion is constrained to a particular group of persons.

Electronic discussions can be extremely useful and professionally rewarding, but they can also be useless. They are guaranteed to be time consuming, and can consume all of your time if you let them. Whether they are useful or useless depends upon a number of variables, only some of which are under your control. For tips on taking control of those variables over which you exert some authority as well as other tips, see "E-Mail Tips & Tricks: Electronic Discussions" in this section.

**LISTSERV Lists**

LISTSERV lists are electronic discussions that are supported by a particular software program called "LISTSERV". This software automates functions related to setting up, moderating, and interacting with electronic discussion lists. The LISTSERV software offers a number of functions for subscribers beyond merely subscribing or unsubscribing to electronic discussions. By using various LISTSERV commands, it is possible to find out who else is subscribed to a particular list, search past messages of archived discussions, and retrieve files if such items have been made available by the discussion moderator. LISTSERV lists have historically been associated with the BITNET network, since all LISTSERV lists are hosted by BITNET nodes.

## Mail Reflectors

Mail reflectors are discussions that are not supported by the LISTSERV software. Many reflectors are simple forwarding devices that take a message in to a central address and forwards copies to a specified list of recipients. Typically, to subscribe to a discussion hosted by a mail reflector it is necessary to send your request to an e-mail address that puts "-request" on the end of the list name. For example, to subscribe to the "wais-discussion" on Wide Area Information Servers, one sends a free-text subscription message to "wais-discussion-request@think.com". Note that if you leave off the "-request" part of the address, your message will be distributed to the entire discussion list and you will annoy a number of people. Generally, mail reflector requests must be handled individually by a human being rather than automatically by software, although increasingly these discussions are becoming automated or semi-automated through software similar to LISTSERV.

## Usenet News

Electronic discussions on Usenet are handled very differently from LISTSERV lists. Instead of "subscribing" to a discussion, after which you receive e-mail messages from the list, Usenet news is broadcast on the net. You dip into it by initiating a session with newsreader software. It is comparable to computer bulletin boards, where you can go to view messages at will rather than have them come to you directly. When Usenet news is an option, many choose it because it saves storage space and costs. For more information, see the Fact Sheet "Usenet News."

## Discussion Topics

There are dozens of electronic discussions that focus on topics in librarianship. Most fall into one of two categories: broad topical discussions or discussions relating to a particular online system. In addition, there are several lists outside of librarianship that librarians may find useful (e.g., the Campus-Wide Information Systems list may be of interest to academic librarians). Beyond these, of course, are thousands of discussions in a multitude of subject areas from A to Z. A selected few include (for examples of the use of commands mentioned here, see the "LISTSERV Command Summary" in this section):

*PACS-L*
As the first such discussion, the Public Access Computer Systems Forum can be considered the "mother of all library lists". At over 4000 subscribers now in dozens of countries around the world, it is by far the largest library discussion. To subscribe, send the message "SUB PACS-L Your Name" to LISTSERV@UHUPVM1.BITNET.

*ARCHIVES*
A list for issues relating to archival collections and archivists. To subscribe, send the message "SUB ARCHIVES Your Name" to: LISTSERV@INDYCMS.BITNET.

*AUTOCAT*
Library Cataloging and Authorities Discussion Group. To subscribe, send the message "SUB AUTOCAT Your Name" to LISTSERV@UVMVM.BITNET.

## Discussion Topics cont'd

**BI-L**

A list for discussing Bibliographic Instruction issues. To subscribe, send the message "SUB BI-L Your Name" to LISTSERV@BINGVMB.BITNET.

**CWIS-L**

The Campus-Wide Information Systems discussion list. To subscribe, send the message "SUB CWIS-L Your Name" to LISTSERV@WUVMD.BITNET.

**GOVDOC-L**

Government documents discussion list. To subscribe, send the message "SUB GOVDOC-L Your Name" to LISTSERV@PSUVM.BITNET.

**LIBADMIN**

Library administration and management issues. To subscribe, send the message "SUB LIBADMIN Your Name" to LISTSERV@UMAB.BITNET.

**LIBREF-L**

A discussion for reference issues. To subscribe, send the message "SUB LIBREF-L Your Name" to LISTSERV@KENTVM.BITNET.

## Directories of Electronic Discussions

For more information on what electronic discussions are available, refer to one or more of these sources:

*Interest Groups list*

The most comprehensive source for discussion lists in existence is the "interest-groups" file maintained by the Network Information Systems Center at SRI International. It is available for anonymous ftp at ftp.nisc.sri.com, in directory "netinfo", with the filename "interest-groups".

*ARL Directory*

The Office of Scientific and Academic Publishing of the Association of Research Libraries publishes a *Directory of Electronic Journals, Newsletters, and Academic Discussion Lists*. The latest edition was released in March 1992. It is comprised of two sections: one on electronic journals and the other on academic discussion lists. The section on academic discussion lists is compiled by Diane Kovacs, who also makes the information available electronically (via anonymous ftp to ksuvxa.kent.edu or via LISTSERV commands to LISTSERV@KENTVM, filenames ACADLIST FILE1 through ACADLIST FILE7, and in other formats).

*Charles Bailey's list*

Charles Bailey, Jr., the founder and former moderator of PACS-L, maintains a list of library discussion lists that is periodically distributed to PACS-L subscribers. It is the best condensed list of library discussions available.

*NEW-LIST*

To find out about new discussion lists as soon as they are created, send the message "SUB NEW-LIST Your Name" to LISTSERV@NDSUVM1.BITNET.

## For More Information

Bailey, Jr., Charles W. "The Public-Access Computer Systems Forum: A Computer Conference on BITNET," *Library Software Review*, 9: 71-74.

Kovacs, Diane K., W. McCarty, and Michael J. Kovacs. "How to Start and Manage a BITNET-Listserv Discussion Group: A Beginner's Guide," *The Public-Access Computer Systems Review*, 2(1) (1991). [Available by e-mail message "GET KOVACS PRV2N1 to LISTSERV@UHUPVM1.BITNET]

Kovacs, Michael J. and Diane K. Kovacs. "The State of Scholarly Electronic Conferencing, " *Electronic Networking: Research, Applications and Policy*, 1(2) (Winter 1991): 29-36.

Rapaport, Matthew. *Computer Mediated Communications: Bulletin Boards, Computer Conferencing, Electronic Mail, and Information Retrieval*. New York: Wiley, 1991.

# LISTSERV Command Summary

**Introduction**

All interaction with a LISTSERV discussion list occurs through the use of a special software program called LISTSERV. This software offers a number of options for both list "owners" and list "subscribers" to interact with the discussion list. These options are discussed in more detail below.

All of the following commands must be sent as electronic mail to the LISTSERV at whatever site (computer node) is the "host" of the particular electronic discussion to which your message refers. For example, if you wish to subscribe to the PACS-L discussion, which is hosted by the computer "UHUPVM1", then you would send your subscription command to LISTSERV@UHUPVM1. If you are sending the message from an Internet-connected computer you will need to add ".BITNET" on the end of the address so it looks like this: LISTSERV@UHUPVM1.BITNET. All other commands relating to the PACS-L list would go to this address as well. Whenever you send a message to the LISTSERV, the subject line should be left blank and the command you wish the LISTSERV to obey should be in the "body" of the message.

**Subscribing**

To subscribe to an electronic discussion, send the following message to the LISTSERV:

SUB *<LIST NAME>* <Your Name>    example: SUB  PACS-L  Roy Tennant

The area following the list name is free text; that is, the LISTSERV will accept anything you wish to enter.

**Unsubscribing**

To unsubscribe to an electronic discussion, send the following message to the LISTSERV:

UNSUB *<LIST NAME>*              example: UNSUB  PACS-L

Please note that when unsubscribing, you should not include your name. The LISTSERV software will remove you from the subscription list based upon the return e-mail address in your e-mail message.

**Suspending Mail**

To temporarily stop the receipt of messages from a list, it is possible to "suspend" your subscription – a particularly handy function for vacations. To do this, send the following message to the LISTSERV:

SET *<LIST NAME>*  NOMAIL      example: SET  PACS-L  NOMAIL

Please note that it is not necessary to specify your name.

## Resuming Mail

To resume mail once you have suspended it (see above), send the following command to the LISTSERV. Please note that this does not send you any back mail, it merely resumes at that point.

SET  <*LIST NAME*>  MAIL          example: SET  PACS-L  MAIL

## Reviewing the Subscriber List

It is possible to receive a list of all the subscribers to a particular electronic discussion who have not specifically requested that their subscription be hidden, unless list policy holds the list private. To retrieve this list, send the following message to the LISTSERV:

REV  <*LIST NAME*>          example: REV  PACS-L

One trick for finding the electronic mail addresses of collegues is to obtain the list of subscribers from a large library list like PACS-L and then search the list for the name you wish to find. See "E-Mail Tips & Tricks: Finding Addresses" for more information.

## Retrieving Files

Some electronic discussions archive past messages or other files. To receive a list of such files, send the following command to the LISTSERV:

INDEX  <*LIST NAME*>          example: INDEX  PACS-L

To retrieve a particular file listed in the INDEX file, send the following message to the LISTSERV:

GET  <*FILE NAME*>  <*FILE TYPE*>    example: GET  LISTSERV  REFCARD

## Searching Archived Lists

Some electronic discussions are archived; that is, past messages are saved for a period of time, often years. If a discussion has been archived, then it can be searched by keyword using a particular search command structure.

*Basic Search*
Below is the syntax and an example for a simple search.

| Syntax: | Example: |
| --- | --- |
| // | // |
| database search dd=rules | database search dd=rules |
| //rules dd   * | //rules dd   * |
| search *KEYWORD* in *LIST NAME* | search internet in PACS-L |
| index | index |
| /* | /* |

*Advanced Searching Options*

Besides a basic keyword search, the LISTSERV software offers additional functionality. It is possible to limit to a particular date range by adding "from YR/MNTH/DAY to YR/MNTH/DAY" on the end of the search statement (for example, "Search Internet in PACS-L from 92/1/1 to 92/6/30"). Or you can specify any messages after a particular date (for example, "Search Internet in PACS-L since 92/1/1"). It is also possible to use the wildcard character "*" to find all the messages posted on a particular day (for example, "Search * in PACS-L from 92/6/30 to 92/6/30"), week, or month. When two search terms are specified, it is treated as a Boolean "and"; that is, the search terms "internet catalog" would retrieve only messages in which both words were found. It is also possible to use the operators OR and NOT in search strings, as well as parentheses for appropriate grouping of terms.

*Retrieving Certain Messages*

Once you have identified the message(s) in which you are interested based upon your search, you need to send a message to the LISTSERV to print those messages specified by the number assigned to each message. To do this, you would send the following message to the LISTSERV:

| Syntax: | Example: |
|---|---|
| // | // |
| database search dd=rules | database search dd=rules |
| //rules dd   * | //rules dd   * |
| search *KEYWORD* in *LIST NAME* | search internet in PACS-L |
| print all of MESSAGE#  MESSAGE# | print all of 2357 3461 3465 |
| /* | /* |

To receive a document that details the possible search commands, sent the message INFO DATABASE to any host running the LISTSERV software (e.g., LISTSERV@BITNIC.BITNET). To discover what other LISTSERV-related documents exist, send the command INFO. The mail message that will be returned to you will list general information files that can be obtained by sending the appropriate GET command to the LISTSERV (e.g., GET LISTSERV REFCARD to retrieve the LISTSERV Command Reference Card). New LISTERV users are advised to retrieve the "Presentation of LISTSERV for New Users" (LISTPRES MEMO) and "General Information About Revised LISTSERV" (LISTSERV MEMO) documents.

# E-Mail Tips & Tricks: Electronic Discussions

**Introduction**

Electronic discussions or "lists" can be interesting, informative and can help you develop professionally. They can also be time-consuming, dull, and even useless. Whether a discussion is in the former category or the latter depends on several factors, some of which are discussed below.

**All discussions are not created equal**

Electronic discussions can be moderated or unmoderated. The distinction is whether the list owner first receives all messages sent to a discussion and weeds out the spurious messages or those sent to the discussion by mistake (as in persons trying to subscribe or unsubscribe) before they are forwarded to the entire list. If the discussion is very closely moderated (e.g., PACS-L), the list owner will combine several messages on the same topic into one message that is then sent out to all subscribers. Unmoderated discussions can sometimes fill your mailbox with routing error messages, messages from readers wishing to subscribe or unsubscribe, or postings that are not appropriate for the discussion (as in broadcast ads for conferences on unrelated topics). In general, then, moderated discussions are much preferred over unmoderated ones.

**Discussion quality varies widely**

Just as all discussions are not created equal, so do they also not achieve an equal "quality of life". A discussion is only as good as those doing the discussing, and each subscriber list is different. Also, you may find that a few subscribers seem to dominate the contributions to the discussion. If those who choose to contribute often do not offer interesting, informative, thoughtful comments or information, then the quality of the discussion suffers. Use your judgment. For your own part, think before you send. Will your message contribute something meaningful to the discussion? Will others find value in it? Refrain from posting messages devoid of added value, such as "I agree" or "How true" postings. Be a good "net citizen."

**All things in moderation**

There are thousands of electronic discussions on a wide range of topics. Just within librarianship there are dozens of discussions that range from discussing the automated system of a particular vendor to all computer systems to which patrons have access and beyond. It is easy – perhaps all too easy – to oversubscribe and become inundated with messages that may or may not be germane to the work at hand. Cultivate a keen sense of when a list is productive professionally for you and when it is not. Unsusbscribe from those that have a lower "signal" (useful messages) to "noise" (useless messages) ratio. A good approach when first subscribing to a list is to consciously watch the quality of the exchange for a while and determine what, if anything you are getting out of it. Feel free to "dip" into discussions to try them out and unsubscribe quickly if they do not meet your needs. Remember that electronic discussions can be attractive and habit forming but that you also have other things to do.

## Cultivate mutual filtering arrangements

An effective method for sifting the wheat from the chaff in electronic discussions is to make arrangements with colleagues to forward items of interest to you from a list to which you do not subscribe. You can offer to do the same for them, provided you each know generally what the other would find of interest. Large group arrangements may be possible, but it becomes much more difficult to determine what would be of interest to someone. The benefit of serendipitious discovery should not be discounted.

## Read discussions via Usenet news

Many Internet sites have access to Usenet news, aka newsgroups, aka readnews. Most BITNET lists of note are gatewayed to Usenet news, which means you can read all postings to an electronic discussion as if they were posted on a bulletin board rather than delivered as personal mail. By initiating a "readnews" session, you can select the bulletin board or discussion that you wish to read and use the increased functionality that the readnews software affords you. For example, if you read a message that did not interest you, you could delete (or mark as "read") all messages that subsequently replied to that message. This way you can delete entire discussion "threads" quickly and easily. As personal mail, you would need to delete each message individually unless they happened to be grouped together in your mailbox – an unlikely occurrence. Readnews software also has other features that may be more useful to you than e-mail discussion lists.

## KISS

"Keep it simple, stupid" is good advice to follow when posting a message to an electronic discussion. State your problem, opinion, advice, or whatever simply and directly. Assume that the people reading your message are just as busy as you are and are just as likely to be frustrated rather than inspired by long-winded, self-important postings. The respect of your colleagues is much more likely to be won by a judicious use of the medium than not.

## Be careful when using the "reply" function

Virtually all e-mail software has a command that allows you to reply quickly and easily to a mail message. The software takes the "From:" field of the message header and reverses it to the "To:" field and puts "Re:" in front of the subject in the "Subject:" field. This is normally a wonderful feature that saves you time and trouble. With mail from electronic discussions, however, it is much more likely to *make trouble*. Since it is so easy to reply to mail, you can reverse a message and send your reply off before realizing to what address, in fact, it is being sent. This is because the "From:" field can have one or more addresses: the address of the *person* who sent the message, or the address of the *electronic discussion* which forwarded it to you. Therefore, if you meant to reply directly to the person who posted the message but the reply function reversed the address of the electronic discussion, you could (and many people do) send a very personal message to thousands of unwitting recipients. Better not to get even *close* to that possibility.

## Be selective

Learn to be selective regarding what you choose to read. If the subject of the message is not something of interest, delete it without reading it. You will find that the time saved can be used more productively in reading and responding to those in which you are interested.

## Give your message a subject

When you initiate an original message (rather than responding to someone else's comment), give it a succinct, descriptive subject. When responding to someone else's original comments or when contributing to a particular topic, use the existing subject. In that way, interested people can follow the development of that discussion without missing your comments.

# Electronic Journals

## Introduction

Electronic journals are a relatively recent yet quickly growing phenomenon. The term "electronic journals" is often used to cover a wide range of serial publication types: newsletters, magazines, peer-reviewed journals, and new kinds of publications to which there is no print counterpart. The ease and rapidity with which documents can be widely transmitted via electronic mail to thousands of subscribers seems custom-made for the delivery of the type of short, timely information that journals typically provide.

Although most electronic journals consist of only text (no graphics, formulas, diagrams, etc.), increasingly information in other formats is being provided. Typically, one subscribes to these publications in ways similar to those used to subscribe to electronic discussions. For those journals that are supported by LISTSERV software, a regular LISTSERV subscription command sent to the appropriate computer is sufficient to receive a journal. For journals distributed via Internet mail, you may need to send a message to a particular address where a person will add your name to the subscription list. Most electronic journals are available free, although recently more journals have begun appearing for which there is a fee to subscribe.

## For More Information

*Public Access Computer Systems Review*, Volume 2, no. 1, 1991. This special issue of the *PACS Review* is devoted to the topic of electronic journals. The Strangelove/Kovacs directory cited below has a synopsis of the articles in this issue and instructions for retrieving the files.

Bailey, Charles W., Jr. "Electronic Publishing on Networks: A Selective Bibliography," *Public Access Computer Systems Review* 3(2) (1992): 13-20.

————. "Network-Based Electronic Serials," *Information Technology and Libraries* 11(1), (March 1992): 29-35.

Strangelove, Michael and Diane Kovacs. *Directory of Electronic Journals, Newsletters and Academic Discussion Lists.* Washington, DC: Association of Research Libraries, 1992. [The electronic journals portion of this document is available by sending the message GET EJOURNL1 DIRECTRY on one line, and GET EJOURNL2 DIRECTRY (note: there is no "a" in EJOURNL and no "o" in DIRECTRY) on another line, to listserv@acadvm1.uottawa.ca.]

# Exercise: Beginners

**The Task**

This exercise is intended to ensure that you are familiar with basic e-mail features.

**The Method**

To do the following exercise, you will need to have the manual for your local e-mail system or consult your local system support personnel. That is because E-mail software varies in the commands used to accomplish e-mail tasks.

*First:*
Form a small group of 2 or 3 people, who will agree to receive your mail exercises and reply to them. In the exercises below, you will be referred to as "A", and your teammates as "B" and "C". If you cannot team up with others, send the messages to yourself.

*For each message you send:*
> In the SUBJECT block, indicate the exercise you are doing—e.g.,
> SUBJECT: Exercise 3—Forwarding

*Practice the following features* (using the commands of your local e-mail software):

1. cc:          Send a message to "B" with copies to "C" and yourself. In the body of the message, ask B to write you a message.

2. bcc:         Send a message to "B" with a blind copy to yourself.

3. forward      Forward to "C" a message you received from "B"

4. reply        When you receive a message from B or C, use your "reply" command for automatic addressing

5. multiple addressees
                Send a single message to B and C simultaneously

6. save         Save a message in your account or on your computer (i.e., outside your electronic "mailbox")

7. send a file  Send a file (as opposed to a message you enter at the time of sending) to B or C.

# Exercise: All Levels

**Note**

This exercise is written for a particular version of the UNIX operating system and its e-mail software. To do this exercise, you may need to refer to the manual for your e-mail software or consult your local system support personnel for the appropriate commands.

**The Problem**

Find the e-mail address of a colleague.

**The Task**

Guess which discussion group(s) your colleague might subscribe to. Then send to the listserv@node for that discussion group the REV (for review) command, which asks for a list of subscribers to that group.

**The Method**

| What you type | What it means |
|---|---|

Note: In this example you're looking for SMITH in a discussion group LIBRARY

1. Type: **mail LISTSERV@INDYCMS.BITNET** [This will mail a message to the LISTSERV software]

2. Subject: **<return>** [No subject is required]
3. In the body of the message:
   **REV LIBRARY  <return>** [This requests the subscriber list of the discussion group LIBRARY]

4. **. <return>** [Put a period on a line by itself]

   [EOT] [System responds "End of Transmission"]

Please note that it will take anywhere from a few minutes to an hour or more for you to receive a response. Variables that affect the amount of time it takes include the amount of network traffic and how heavily the remote computer is being used. Eventually, you should receive two messages:
- an e-mail message that tells how the job went
- the actual output file, which will consist of the list of subscribers for that list, or in the case of some lists, the summary information (not all lists allow you to retrieve the entire list of subscribers).

When the file arrives in your e-mailbox,
- save it as a file in your computer account, or
- if the file is of manageable size, download it to your PC and search it with whatever string-searching method you have, for example, use the UNIX "grep" command or your word processing software.

In UNIX environment, continue with the next steps to find Smith's address:

5. [wait a minute] [give a little time for the file to reach your account]

6. % **mail** [At the % prompt, re-enter the mail program to find the subscriber list file, and note message number]

7. & **s [#] [filename]** [Save message number as (your-file-name) in your account]

8. & **quit** [Exit mail program]
9. % **ls** [List the files in the directory]
10. % **grep -i smith [filename]** [Search for the string *smith*, upper or lower case, in the file specified]

# Exercise: Advanced Levels

**Note**

This exercise is written for a particular version of the UNIX operating system and its e-mail software. To do this exercise, you may need to refer to the manual for your e-mail software or consult your local system support personnel for the appropriate commands.

**The Problem**

When you returned from vacation, you resumed your subscription to your favorite discussion group PACS-L and entered into the middle of an interesting exchange of ideas about the next generation of OPACs. You want to retrieve all the messages pertaining to that exchange that you missed.

**The Task**

Retrieve all the messages on that topic from the discussion group.

**The Method**

| What you type | What it means |
| --- | --- |

1. Type: **mail LISTSERV@UHUPVM1.BITNET**  [This will mail a message to the LISTSERV software]

2. Subject:    **<return>**  [No subject is required]
3. In the body of the message:

```
//                              [This is your search]
database search dd=rules
//rules dd  *
search generation opac in PACS-L since 92/6/1
index
/*
```

4.  . **<return>**  [Enter a period on a line by itself]

You will get back two messages:
- an e-mail message that tells how the job went
- the actual output file, called DATABASE OUTPUT, which lists by Item # all the messages on your subject

5. % **mail**  [Enter the mail subsytem to read the mail you have received]

6. Choose the item #(s) you want to see and send a second message to the listserv as follows:

```
//
database search dd=rules
//rules dd  *
search generation opac in PACS-L since 92/6/1
print all of <item# item# etc.>
/*
```

**For more information**

To get more complete instructions, send the following message to the listserv address (not to the address for sending discussion messages):
    INFO DATABASE

# E | Internet Remote Login (Telnet)

## This section contains:

- Introduction to Remote Login
- Telnet Command Summary
- Telnet Tips & Tricks
- Exercises

# Introduction to Remote Login

**Introduction**

The remote login function is provided by the Telnet protocol, which is a part of the TCP/IP protocol suite. Telnet allows a network user to connect to a remote computer and use it as if the local computer were a terminal of the remote machine. In using e-mail or FTP your local system essentially moderates your interaction with remote machines. In an interactive Telnet session however, once the connection has been made the local system becomes transparent and you work as if you were directly attached to the remote system. For this reason this capability is sometimes called "interactive connection."

There are two logically distinct capabilities of remote login:

1. While connected to a network machine with Telnet capabilities you can login remotely to any other machine that you have prior permission to use – that is, for which you have a username (login ID) and a password – and use it as you would locally or through "dial-up" access. This includes many commercial services such as DIALOG, RLIN, or OCLC.

2. While connected to a network machine you can login to and then examine remote databases such as online public access catalogs (OPACs), campus-wide information systems (CWIS), and so on. Sometimes a public login ID and password are required. Telnet access to these networked information sources is usually set up so that you can use the remote machine only for searching the database. Accordingly, access usually does not require you to have any special permission and the login procedure is automatic. In some cases you will be denied access to services of the remote machine which are licensed for local use only.

**rlogin**

*rlogin* is a program that allows UNIX machines (running 4.3 BSD) to establish a virtual terminal connection using TCP/IP. Therefore it is analogous to Telnet, but passes UNIX specific information between UNIX machines.

**Using Telnet**

Before starting a Telnet session you'll need the following:
- access to a local machine providing the Telnet service;
- the internet *name or address* of the computer you're trying to reach – this is where guides such as those listed in the "Bibliography" in *Important Information for Beginners* are essential.
- knowledge of some basic commands – as described below.

To connect to a remote machine on the Internet, enter the command "telnet <machine name or numeric address>" from your networked computer. For example entering:

```
telnet 192.35.222.222
```

connects you to the UC MELVYL Library Catalog (see "Names and Addresses"

## Using Telnet
### cont'd

in the section *Internetworking Overview* for more information). If you have an account on the remote machine, or if it is open access (like many library catalogs, including MELVYL), then you may use the remote host as if your local computer were hard-wire connected. To quit, use whatever logoff command the remote system provides. Local implementations of Telnet may vary, so check with your local computer center if you have problems.

Optionally, you may begin Telnet without specifying a machine, usually by entering **telnet** as the command. At this point you may issue various commands, including one to "open" a telnet session with a remote computer, from the Telnet prompt. For example, the following command from the Telnet prompt would also connect you to the UC MELVYL catalog:

```
TELNET> open melvyl.ucop.edu
```

# Telnet Command Summary

**Note**

Though most implementations of Telnet will be similar to commands given here, these examples are taken from UNIX-based Telnet.

**Introduction**

If you enter **telnet** without a machine address, the Telnet service will be initiated and you will see the "TELNET>" prompt. Enter "?" and you will receive a list of Telnet commands. If you are in the middle of a Telnet session and would like to use one of the commands below, you must first "escape" out to the "telnet>" prompt. To do this, you enter an escape sequence (often "CTRL ]", but check your settings by entering "display").

**Commands**

**open <machine address>**
establishes a connection to a remote machine. The machine address may be specified with either the domain name address (e.g., pac.carl.org) or the numeric IP address (e.g., 192.54.81.128).

**close**
closes a connection to a remote machine

**quit**
exits TELNET

**display**
displays your session parameters

**set <parameter>**
sets session parameters (e.g. "set escape <key>" will set a key as the escape command)

**mode**
allows you to enter line-by-line or character-at-a-time mode

**send**
transmits special characters ('send ?' for more)

**status**
prints status information

**toggle**
toggles operating parameters ('toggle ?' for more)

**z**
suspends telnet

**?**
prints help information

**Remember that a remote session can be interrupted with an escape command, often by holding down the control key and hitting the right bracket (]) key.**

# Telnet Tips & Tricks

## How to act like something you're not

Some remote systems require that your computer emulate (act like) a certain terminal type. For example, some systems work best when your computer emulates a VT100 terminal. Other systems may support a wide range of terminal types. IBM systems often require that you use a particular version of Telnet called "tn3270" that allows your computer to act like an IBM 3270 terminal. To connect to these systems you need to have tn3270 available and would use it in place of the the telnet command (e.g., `tn3270 <machine name or numeric address>`). Because this emulation assigns particular values to keys on your keyboard, you should obtain a copy of the key assignments or "map" which is usually available wherever you find tn3270.

## Ports

Occasionally a remote host will require a "port" number in addition to the machine address to insure that you connect properly. These port numbers, when required, are listed with the information about the remote system and are just appended to the initial telnet or open command. For example, the University of Michigan "Weather Underground" service requires you to request port 3000 as in the following:

```
TELNET> open downwind.sprl.umich.edu 3000
```

## Troubleshooting

Several problems occur frequently enough to deserve forewarning. Though Telnet error messages are usually informative and understandable, you should be prepared for the following messages:

• *Unknown host* - Either your network was not able to turn a machine name, e.g. HOLLIS.HARVARD.EDU, into a numeric address, or you mistyped the name or address. Try to reissue the command using the numeric address.

• *Connection refused* - The remote computer is either not functioning properly or cannot accommodate another session – especially likely for heavily used systems (during business hours at the remote site).

• *Connection Dropped* - A problem with the network or the remote host caused the session to be terminated. Unfortunately your only recourse is to start the procedure over again, perhaps waiting a few minutes (or hours!) for the problem to be corrected.

The backspace and carriage return/line feed characters may not be recognized by some systems. Use the local Telnet "set" command or "set ?" to see which key serves as the backspace.

Another common problem is being unable to figure out how to logoff of the remote system. If it is not otherwise obvious, try the commonly used commands "quit," "exit," "bye," "end," "logout," and "logoff". As a last resort you can use the almost universal Telnet escape character mentioned on the next page and then issue the Telnet "close" command. This sometimes leaves the remote system thinking you are still logged on and should be used when nothing else works.

## When all else fails, escape!

It may be useful or necessary to give commands to the Telnet program running on your local machine during a remote session. For example, you might want to check the status of the session. To this end the Telnet software allows a special escape character to be defined, often Ctrl-] or Ctrl-^, which when entered is not simply passed on to the remote system but is interpreted by Telnet to mean that the connection must be temporarily suspended. This will return you to the Telnet prompt from which you can issue Telnet commands, including the close and quit commands. Thus it is a reliable way to finish a remote session which appears to be stuck or when you can discover no other means to escape.

# Exercise: All Levels

**Note**

Though most implementations of Telnet will be similar to commands given here, these examples are taken from UNIX-based Telnet.

**Practice in using remote online catalogs and information files**

This exercise is intended to give you an idea of the variety of information you can retrieve from remote databases. [Note to trainers: In a hands-on class, add the following instructions here: "Half of the class will be assigned to search in Subgroup A for about 15 minutes, and half in Subgroup B; then you will switch groups and search for 15 minutes more. We will then regroup and discuss your results and any problems you may have encountered."]

1. Pick a file from either Subgroup A or Subgroup B.

2. Follow whatever search instructions and help screens are offered online.

> **Trainers: Insert this here**
> 3. Make notes about your observations: ease or difficulty of use; success or failure in finding what you need; etc. Plan to briefly describe your observations to the group.
>
> 4. After about 15 minutes, Subgroup A searchers will choose from Subgroup B list, and Subgroup B searchers will choose from the Subgroup A list.

**LOGIN**
Enter the command "telnet <domain name or numeric address>". If additional login procedures are called for, follow instructions.

**QUIT**
Use whatever logoff command the remote system provides. You may have to try your guesses: for example: quit, logoff, logout, exit, end

**Subgroup A:
ONLINE
CATALOGS**

Choose a subject, author, title, or other bibliographic element appropriate to the file you will search. *Pick something of personal interest to you.*

## United States Online Catalogs

1. Univ. of California 9-campus statewide catalog:
   **MELVYL catalog**
   type: telnet melvyl.ucop.edu or 192.35.222.222

2. **Harvard University** (NOTIS)
   type: telnet 128.103.60.31
   at "Mitek Server..." press ENTER or RETURN
   at the prompt, type: hollis

3. **Univ. of Nebraska** (INNOPAC)
   type: telnet 129.93.16.1
   at login, type: library

4. **New York Public Library**
   type: telnet nyplgate.nypl.org
   at login, type: nypl

5. **Occidental College**
   (has extensive video collection)
   type:  telnet oasys.lib.oxy.edu
   at the resource prompt, type: oasys
   at the login prompt, type: oasys

## International Online Catalogs

1. University of Konstanz, **Germany** (in German)
   type: telnet polydos.uni-konstanz.de 775
   to exit, type: ende

2. The Technion, **Israel** (in English)
   type: telnet lib.technion.ac.il
   at the Username prompt, type: aleph
   at the Terminal type prompt, type: 2

3. Universidad de las Americas, Pueblas, **Mexico** (in Spanish)
   type: telnet bibes.pue.udlap.mx
   at the Username prompt, type: library

4. Karolinska Institute, **Sweden** (in English)
   type: telnet kibib.kib.ki.se
   at the Username prompt, type: library

1. Full text databases at **Dartmouth**
   Shakespeare Plays, Shakespeare Sonnets, The Bible
   type: telnet lib.dartmouth.edu
   Choose the file you want with "select file" command. Try "select file
   shakespeare plays" or "select file shakespeare sonnets"

2. CHOICE book reviews, or
   A guide to the Internet, or
   Reference sources
   via **Colorado Alliance of Research Libraries (CARL)**
   type: telnet pac.carl.org
   (Once in the catalog, choose "Information databases.")

**Subgroup B:
SPECIAL
DATABASES
cont'd**

3.  Agricultural information
    International export and trade information
    via **Cal State Fresno Campus Information Network**
    type: telnet caticsuf.csufresno.edu
    login: public

4.  A variety of public and community information
    via several **Freenet** systems (based on Cleveland FreeNet)
    type:  telnet heartland.bradley.edu   [for the Heartland FreeNet]
              login: bbguest          or
           telnet 129.137.100.1  [for Tri-State Online]
              login: visitor              or
           telnet yfn.ysu.edu    [for Youngstown FreeNet]
              login: visitor

5.  World news
    Weather
    Dictionary
    Thesaurus
    CIA World Factbook
    via **Rutgers University Campus Information Network**
    type: telnet info.rutgers.edu

6.  Space information for K-12 educators and students:
    Information about shuttle launches
    Astronauts' biographies
    NASA publications
    via **SpaceLink**
    type: telnet spacelink.msfc.nasa.gov

7.  Weather/earthquake information from the Dept. of Atmospheric, Oceanic &
    Space Sciences.
    Forecasts for major US and Canadian cities
    Ski conditions
    Earthquake reports
    via **U of M Weather Underground**
    type: telnet downwind.sprl.umich.edu 3000

8.  **NETFIND**
    Given the name of a person on the Internet and a rough address of where the
    person works, Netfind attempts to locate their e-mail address.
    type: telnet bruno.cs.colorado.edu
    login: netfind

9.  **National Science Foundation Information Service**
    Provides access to the entire range of information, grant opportunities, etc.
    published by the NSF.
    type: telnet stis.nsf.gov
    login: public
    type: vt100nkp [or experiment with other types if that doesn't work]

**Subgroup B:
SPECIAL
DATABASES
cont'd**

10. Genetics database
Provides access to gene sequence information. Users enter questions in plain English, retrieve a list of documents, and select documents from the list for reading or printing.
via **GenBank**
type: telnet genbank.bio.net
login: genbank
password: 4nigms

11. Agriculturally-oriented database from Pennsylvania State University
Includes information ranging from cattle to agricultural prices to weather.
via **PENpages**
type: telnet psupen.psu.edu
login: pnotpa

12. U.S. Postal Service and U.S. Geodetic Survey data
Zip code, telephone area code, time zone
Elevation and Latitude/Longitude
Population
via **Geographic Name Server**
type: telnet martini.eecs.umich.edu 3000

13. Virtual reality Vision of the 24th century
Science Center of Interactive Exhibits
Tour the planets and stars in a pilotable starship
via **MicroMuse—Electronic Village**
type: telnet chezmoto.ai.mit.edu 4201

14. Try out a **Gopher** system (see the Fact Sheet section for more info)
type: telnet consultant.micro.umn.edu
login: gopher

15. **Sonoma State University's** menu-driven system for providing access to online systems via the Internet (for more information, see the Fact Sheet on LIBS)
type: telnet vax.sonoma.edu
login: LIBS

16. **University of Maryland Info Database**
type: telnet info.umd.edu
login: info

17. **University of North Carolina's Internet Extended Bulletin Board Service**
telnet bbs.oit.unc.edu or 152.2.22.80

# Notes

# F | Internet File Transfer (FTP)

*This section contains:*

- Introduction to FTP
- FTP Command Summary
- Downloading & Translating Files
- FTP Tips & Tricks
- Common FTP File Extensions
- Exercises

# Introduction to FTP

**Introduction**

The process of transferring files from one Internet-connected computer to another is handled by the File Transfer Protocol, or FTP. This protocol is defined by network protocol documents within the Request for Comments (RFC) series (refer to the *Fact Sheets* section for more information on RFCs). What network protocol documents define, however, is a low-level description of how the computers are to interact to allow this transfer to take place. The user interface, or the commands that a network user must utilize to transfer files, is not well defined by these documents. Instead, a common command set has evolved that most computers understand and support. In addition, there are numerous other methods that network users can use to transfer files using the file transfer protocol. For example, there are several Macintosh-based graphical user interfaces that make transferring files a snap. What is outlined in this section is the common command set that most network users must still use, but please be aware that implementations vary.

**Anonymous FTP**

To transfer files from one computer to another it is necessary to connect to the computer with which you wish to transfer files. Normally you would only be allowed to connect to a computer upon which you have an account, but some computer administrators have set aside areas on their machines that can be accessed anonymously (without an account) for the purpose of distributing documents, software, and other files. This is commonly called "anonymous FTP", and it is a service of the Internet that anyone connected to the Internet may use. Computer administrators who offer files for anonymous file transfer are providing a public service. Please exercise restraint in connecting to these machines. Stay away from "prime time" hours (6:00 am to 7:00 pm at the remote site) when the demand on their computing resources is likely the highest.

To use anonymous FTP, your computer must be connected to the Internet. Enter the command:

> ftp <computer name or number>    *example:* `ftp hydra.uwo.ca`

When you are prompted for a login, enter:

> anonymous                *example:* `anonymous`

When you are prompted for a password, enter:

> your e-mail address      *example:* `rtennant@library.berkeley.edu`

You should now be connected to the remote computer and can use FTP commands to look at the directories and transfer files (refer to "FTP Command Summary"). To obtain a list of available FTP commands, enter "help".

**Sample FTP Session**

The following is a sample FTP session. The commands entered by the user are in bold type. The file being retrieved is an executable file (Ernest Perez's hypertext version of the document *Library Resources on the Internet: Strategies for Selection and Use*) and therefore is being transferred in binary mode. Refer to "Common FTP File Extensions" for information on which files require binary mode.

**Sample FTP Session** cont'd

```
% ftp hydra.uwo.ca
Connected to hydra.uwo.ca.
Name (hydra.uwo.ca:rtennant): anonymous
331 anonymous user ok. Send real ident as password.
Password: rtennant@library.berkeley.edu
230-Guest User RTENNANT@LIBRARY.BERKELEY.EDU logged into PUB:[000000]
at Wed  3-Jun-92 15:33, job e8d.
230 Directory and access restrictions apply
ftp> cd libsoft
250 Connected to PUB:[000000.LIBSOFT].
ftp> binary
200 Type I ok.
ftp> get libinet.exe
200 Port 9.9 at Host 128.32.159.12 accepted.
150 IMAGE retrieve of PUB:[000000.LIBSOFT]LIBINET.EXE;1 started.
226 Transfer completed.  248760 (8) bytes transferred.
local: libinet.exe remote: libinet.exe
248760 bytes received in 59 seconds (4.1 Kbytes/s)
ftp> quit
221 QUIT command received. Goodbye.
```

## How to Find the File You Need

Often when you use anonymous FTP, it will be to retrieve a file that you know exists at a particular archive site. Sometimes, however, you may need to find a file that you know exists or you think exists, but for which you have no access information. There are several ways to locate the file you need.

*Check a bibliography*, such as Deirdre Stanton's *Using Networked Information Resources* bibliography, which includes FTP access information for files cited.

*Ask a colleague.* Sometimes a colleague will know where to locate the file, or perhaps may have already retrieved it.

*Look in  the major network archive sites:*

| Source for: | Sites: |
| --- | --- |
| network information, RFCs | ftp.nisc.sri.com |
|  | nnsc.nsf.net |
|  | nic.ddn.mil |
| microcomputer software, etc. | wuarchive.wustl.edu |
| Macintosh software, etc. | sumex-aim.stanford.edu |
| library-related files | hydra.uwo.ca |
|  | infolib.murdoch.edu.au |
|  | ftp.unt.edu |
|  | ftp.cni.org |

*Search an Archie server.* Archie is a database of the names and locations of thousands of programs contained within hundreds of FTP archive sites around the world. By connecting to Archie and searching on a filename or a portion of a filename, you can locate files that match your search and where they are located. To search Archie, TELNET to archie.ans.net or 147.225.1.2. There are also other Archie sites in locations around the world. Login as "archie" and enter "help" for more information on searching the database. For more information, see the "Archie" fact sheet in the *Fact Sheets* section.

# FTP Command Summary

The commands below are a common set of commands for transferring files using FTP. Please be aware that these commands are not standard and implementations may vary.

**Commands**

`ftp <machine address>`
establishes an FTP session with the named machine. The machine address may be specified with either the domain name address (e.g., sumex-aim.stanford.edu) or the numeric IP address (e.g., 36.44.0.6)

`ls`
lists the files and directories in the current directory

`cd <directory name>`
changes the directory to the one named. If the directory named is not a subdirectory of the current directory, then the path (e.g., cd /pub/library) must be specified

`get <filename>`
transfers the remote file specified by "filename" to your local computer. To change the name of the file on your local computer, add the local filename to the end of the command (e.g., get remotefile localfile)

`binary`
changes the transfer mode from text or ASCII (default setting) to binary. This is required before transferring files of particular types (see handout on file extensions for more information)

`ascii`
changes the transfer mode to straight text.

`help`
lists available FTP commands

`quit`
disconnects from the remote machine and quits FTP

`mget  <characters*>`
"muliple get" – By using the wildcard character "*" this command transfers all files that match the filename characters specified (e.g., the command "mget *.txt" would retrieve all files with the extension ".txt") from the remote computer to your local computer

`cdup`
changes the current directory to the "parent" directory, or the one above it (therefore "up" in the hierarchy)

## Commands
### cont'd

**dir**
lists the files and directories in the current directory, showing sizes of the files and other information

**put <filename>**
transfers the file specified from your local computer to the remote computer. This operation requires special authorization.

**mput <characters*>**
"multiple put" – works like "mget" above only for transferring files from your local computer to the remote computer

**lcd <directory name>**
changes your current directory on your *local* computer

**prompt**
toggles interactive prompting during mget and mput commands. If interactive prompting is turned on, you will be asked to confirm each file transferred

**pwd**
prints (displays) the name of the current working directory on the remote machine

**bye**
synonym for quit

**remotehelp**
requests help from the remote FTP server. If a command name is also specified (for example, remotehelp cdup), it is supplied to the server as well

# Downloading & Translating Files

**Introduction**

You may not be in a position to have your personal computer directly connected to the Internet. If this is the case, to gain access to the Internet, you must either dialup using SLIP (Serial Line Internet Protocol, see the *Fact Sheet*) or login to an account on another computer – often a workstation, minicomputer or mainframe – that is on the Internet. In the latter case, when a file is retrieved via FTP, the file will reside on the workstation or minicomputer, *not* your personal computer. Therefore, in order to get the file to your PC (PC is used here to denote all types and brands of personal computer), you must *download* the file from the Internet-connected computer to your PC using communications software and a file transfer protocol. Presumably, you already possess a modem and communications software in order to even connect to the Internet-connected computer in the first place, so we will discuss below what is required to download and translate a file beyond those basic requirements.

Please note that if your personal computer is directly connected to the Internet or connected via SLIP software, you will not need to download files that you retrieve via FTP. However, you may need to translate them depending upon the file format.

**Downloading**

Downloading is the process of transferring a file from a larger computer to a smaller one, usually a minicomputer or mainframe to a personal computer, usually through serial or phone lines. To accomplish this, both computers must use a common file transfer protocol, which is an agreement on exactly how the file transfer is to take place. There are numerous file transfer protocols, with a couple of the more common being Kermit and Xmodem or its variants. You should check your PC communications software and with your mainframe computer administrator to see what file transfer protocols are supported.

Different PC communications software have different command sequences for downloading files. Check your documentation or help screens for information on what those commands are. Typically, you dialup the computer from which you wish to download a file, login to your account, and enter the mainframe command to start the file transfer. If you wish to download a binary file, you will need to specify that in your mainframe command. Then you enter the command on your PC to initiate the downloading function. Your PC software will prompt you to select the file transfer protocol you wish to use (presuming you have a choice) and to enter where you want the file to be stored (what drive and directory) and what you wish to name it. Once that is done, your PC sends a signal that you do not see to the remote computer that it can commence sending the file. As the file is sent, your PC communications software may display to you how it is going and if any errors have been detected. When the transfer is complete, you will usually be notified somehow (some programs beep at you). The file should then be on your PC (or floppy disk if you specified that location).

## Translating

If the file you retrieved and downloaded is not a straight text file it may need to be "translated" from one format (e.g., compressed) to another (e.g., uncompressed). Special programs are often needed to perform this operation, although "self-extracting archives" (see below) are an exception. The translation programs usually required to make a file useable are often available in the same locations that offer files for anonymous file transfer. Often they are in a "utilities" directory under the operating system to which they refer (e.g., DOS, Macintosh). Please see "Common FTP File Extensions" in this section as a place to start for identifying which programs are required to translate the commonly used file formats.

Self-extracting archives are files that have been compressed, but do not require special software to uncompress them. All you do is execute the file (in DOS, enter the name of the file when in the same directory, on a Mac double-click on it) and it will extract itself. These kinds of files are usually a number of separate files that have been compresed together in a unit, so it is best to make sure the file is in its own directory (for DOS) or in a separate folder (for Mac) before running it. Common file extensions for self-extracting archives are "sea" for Mac files and "exe" for DOS files (although this extension could also denote other types of executable files).

## Special Notes

*Postscript Files*
Postscript files are documents that have been translated to a format that any Postcript-compatible printer can print in the original form (with all formatting, figures, etc. intact). These files are generated by "printing" a document to a file rather than to a printer, and they consist of the text of the document plus formatting commands in a language that all Postscript printers can process. Although the document is basically unreadable in this format due to the presence of a large number of special codes, the file is nonetheless a straight ASCII text file and can be transferred and downloaded in text mode.

*tar.Z Files*
Many Internet FTP archive sites are maintained on UNIX computers, and the administrators of these sites will often combine and compress the files using the UNIX programs "tar" and "compress". You can determine if a particular file has been processed in this manner by the extensions "tar.Z" at the end of a filename (refer to "Common FTP Filename Extensions" in this section). Tar stands for "tape archive," and is used primarily to combine several files and/or files and directories into one file. "Z" denotes that the file has been compressed with the UNIX compress command in order to save disk space. To decompress a "tar.Z" file, first enter "uncompress [filename]" where filename is the file you wish to uncompress, including the "tar.Z" extension. To "untar" a file enter "tar -fx [filename]" where [filename] is the file you wish to untar as well as the "tar" extension. Please note that UNIX implementations vary, so check your local documentation if you have difficulty. Also, PC-based programs exist at FTP archive sites to accomplish these tasks.

# FTP Tips & Tricks

**Become familiar with key archives**

There are several archive sites that are important sources for network documents (RFCs, etc.) and general purpose software, and other archive sites that are important sources for library-related information and software. Most files that you need will tend to show up in these key locations. Become familiar with a couple of the ones that you find most helpful, so that you need not constantly relearn the directory structure and conventions (whether an index or README file (see below) is available in each directory, etc.) that apply to those particular archive sites. If you do not use them often, you may wish to create a brief "cheat sheet" that describes the directory structure, whether index or readme files exist and where they are located. Alternatively, print some selected directory listings.

**Check your key archive sites for new files periodically**

If you have identified a select few sites that often have files of interest to you, it is not too difficult to connect occasionally and check for interesting new files. Site administrators tend to add files on a regular basis, but only occasionally announce new additions to the Internet at large through electronic discussions or other means.

**Read the "README" file**

The "README" file, if it exists, has that name for a reason: it will often tell you important information about the archive site or the files within a subdirectory.

**Use a paging facility to read files you don't need to transfer**

If your local computer system has the ability to display large text files a screen at a time (also called a paging facility), such as "more" or "less" (in some UNIX operating systems, it is not necessary to retrieve a file to display it. Simply "pipe" (redirect) it to the paging facility like this:

```
get README |more
```

Unlike an unpiped "get" command, when you quit out of the paging facility, the file is not in your local computer account. Instead you can think of it as being transferred to your screen.

**Remember to use binary mode when necessary**

The default mode for FTP is ASCII, or text, mode. It is often all too easy to forget to enter "binary" at the FTP prompt to change to binary mode before transferring files such as software programs, some compressed files, etc. Refer to "Common FTP File Extensions" for tips on what files require binary mode.

**Look for INDEX files in large directories**

FTP site directories that include a large number of files will sometimes offer an INDEX file to assist users in identifying the file they need. Such a file can then be retrieved and searched, viewed or printed so you can find out exactly which file(s) you wish to obtain. If you have a paging facility (see above) that supports searching (such as "less" or "more"), you can use it to search the file without actually transferring it to your local machine.

**If at first you don't succeed, try again**

If you receive the message that a file you tried to transfer does not exist, first check to make sure that you are entering the correct filename *and* extension, if one exists. Filenames are often *case sensitive*, which means you must match the upper and lowercase characters of the filename exactly. Please note that your local computer may require you to enter a filename for the local copy of the file. For example, you may need to enter:

```
ftp remote.file local.file
```

which specifies both the name of the file on the remote computer and what you wish the name of the local file to be. In addition, your local operating system may require that the local filename adhere to certain naming conventions. Generally it is better to use short file names (8 characters or less).

**When all else fails, explore**

Sometimes you fail to transfer a file because you do not realize that you are in the wrong directory on the remote machine. Enter an "ls" command to list the files in the current directory. If the file you think should be there is not listed, move up the directory hierarchy (if you are not already at the top) by entering "cdup" for "change directory up". Then make sure you change to the appropriate subdirectory. By alternately using the "cd <directory name>" (change directory) and "ls" commands, you can explore a system without knowing ahead of time what is available.

# Common FTP File Extensions

**Introduction**

Internet anonymous FTP archive sites use comon naming conventions to help network users identify file types. The following common filename extensions will help you to identify in which operating system the file was created and usually which file utility or utilities you may need to translate or decompress the file once it is transferred.

The operating system specified in the table below signifies the most likely native operating system of the file; however, it is often possible for decompression programs in other operating systems to appropriately decompress the file. Therefore please note that only a representative example of the required translation program is specified here (whenever possible the most widely available program will be listed). Translation and decompression programs can be found in most major anonymous FTP archive sites. To obtain a more thorough guide to file extensions and the programs required to translate certain formats, retrieve the document "compression" from ftp.cso.uiuc.edu (128.174.5.59) in directory "/doc/pcnet".

**Translation Table**

| Filename Extension | Operating System | Binary or ASCII | Example of program that can translate the file |
|---|---|---|---|
| arc | DOS | B | arc 6.02, pk361 |
| com | DOS | B | executable file — *no trans. required* |
| cpt | Mac | A | Compactor 1.21 |
| doc | any | A | text file — *no translation required* |
| exe | DOS | B | executable file — *no trans. required* |
| hqx | Mac | A | BinHex 4.0 |
| pit | Mac | A | PackIt3.1.3 |
| ps | any | A | send to PostScript printer - *no translation required* |
| sea | Mac | A | self-extracting archive |
| sh | UNIX | A | unshar (UNIX command) |
| sit | Mac | A | Stuffit, Stuffit Deluxe, etc. |
| tar | UNIX | B | tar (UNIX command) |
| txt | any | A | text file — *no translation required* |
| uu | UNIX | A | uudecode (UNIX command) |
| wp | DOS | B | WordPerfect file - *no trans. required* |
| Z | UNIX | B | uncompress (UNIX command) |
| zip | DOS | B | PKZIP/PKUNZIP |

# Exercise: All Levels

**Note**

This exercise is written for a particular version of the UNIX operating system and its implementation of FTP commands. To do this exercise, you may need to refer to your local documentation or consult your local system support personnel for the appropriate commands.

**The Problem**

You want to obtain "There's Gold in Them Thar Networks!," cited in the following PACS-L message:

"...Hitchhiker's Guide to the Internet is fairly technical, and not, as one might expect, a navigational tool. Another RFC, "There's Gold in Them Thar Networks! or Searching for Treasure in all the Wrong Places" (RFC 1290, Dec. 1991: FYI: 10), by Jerry Martin is more helpful."

**The Task**

**If you are advanced**, obtain the document without reading further.

**If you are a beginner**, obtain the document by following the instructions under "The method" below.

**The Method**

The author's instructions above leave out essential steps. As you become more familiar with FTP, you will figure these things out by trial and error. Here are sample instructions for a basic implementation of FTP in a UNIX operating system.

| What you type | What it means |
|---|---|
| 1. Type: **ftp nis.nsf.net** | [This will establish an FTP connection with the "nis.nsf.net" computer] |
| 2. Name: **anonymous** | [login as "anonymous"] |
| 3. Password: **guest** | [usually you would use your actual e-mail address] |
| 4. Type: **cd documents/rfc** | [this specifies the appropriate directory] |
| 5. Type: **get rfc1290.txt** | [this retrieves the file] |
| 6. Type: **quit** | [this exits FTP] |
| 7. Type: **ls** | [to see the file in your account] |
| 8. Type: **more rfc1290.txt** | [to display the file one screen at a time] |
| 9. Type: **q** | [to stop viewing the file] |

# Exercise: Beginner's Level

**Note**

This exercise is written for a particular version of the UNIX operating system and its implementation of FTP commands. To do this exercise, you may need to refer to your local documentation or consult your local system support personnel for the appropriate commands.

**The Problem**

**Add your name to a directory.**

You read this message on the network:

"I have come upon a database of address of Internet users....If you are wondering if a given person has an Internet address, check the DDN Network Information Center (DDN NIC) Its address is nic.ddn.mil. If you want to enter your address onto this database, get a registration form by ftp from nic.ddn.mil, directory netinfo, file user-template.txt.

"If as many users as possible enter the database, the directory will be that much more complete..."

**The Task**

Retrieve the registration form. (You may also wish to take this opportunity to register)

**The Method**

| What you type | What it means |
|---|---|
| 1. Type: **ftp nic.ddn.mil** | [This will establish an FTP connection with the "nis.nsf.net" computer] |
| 2. Name: **anonymous** | [login as "anonymous"] |
| 3. Password: **guest** | [usually you would use your actual e-mail address] |
| 4. Type: **cd netinfo** | [this specifies the appropriate directory] |
| 5. Type: **get user-template.txt** | [this retrieves the file] |
| 6. Type: **quit** | [this exits FTP] |
| 7. Type: **ls** | [to see the file in your account] |
| 8. Type: **more user-template.txt** | [to view it] |
| 9. Type: **q** | [to stop viewing the file] |

# Exercise: Advanced Level

| | |
|---|---|
| **Problem 1** | Find a file in different formats |
| **The Task** | How many different formats of Brendan Kehoe's "Zen and the Art of the Internet" can you find? |
| **Problem 2** | You've written a useful guide for finding ecological information on the Internet and are tired of e-mailing it to the countless individuals who request it weekly. |
| **The Task** | How would you go about making your document available via anonymous ftp? |

# G | Fact Sheets

*This section contains:*

- Archie
- BITNET
- Freenets
- Gopher
- HYTELNET
- Internet
- LIBS
- Project Gutenberg
- Requests for Comments (RFCs)
- SLIP (Serial Line Internet Protocol)
- Usenet News
- Wide Area Information Servers (WAIS)
- World-Wide Web ($W^3$)
- Z39.50 Standard for Information Retrieval

# Archie

**What**

The "archie" service originally began as a searchable database of the files available at several hundred Internet anonymous FTP archive sites. Archie tracks the contents of over 900 separate sites around the world that contain over a million files, updating the list of files in its database for each site about once a month. Besides this service, archie now includes a "whatis" database. This is a database of descriptions of over 3,500 public domain software packages, data sets and informational documents. Other types of information will be added to the whatis database in the future.

**Who**

Archie was developed by:

UNIX Support Group
Computing Centre
McGill University
Room 200, Burnside Hall
805 Sherbrooke Street West
Montreal, Quebec
CANADA   H3A 2K6
(514) 398-3709

Bug reports or suggestions for software changes should be sent to the list of archie implementers: archie-l@archie.mcgill.ca.

**Where**

There are a number of sites that offer archie servers:

| | |
|---|---|
| archie.mcgill.ca | [Canada – the original site] |
| archie.ans.net | |
| archie.au | [Australia] |
| archie.doc.ic.ac.uk | [United Kingdom] |
| archie.rutgers.edu | |
| archie.unl.edu | |
| cs.huji.ac.il | [Israel] |
| archie.funet.fi | [Finland] |
| archie.ncu.edu.tw | [Taiwan] |

Login as "archie", no password is required. Enter "help" for information on searching the database.

**For More Information**

**Electronic Discussion**

There is an electronic discussion list for people interested in archie developments. Send a message to archie-people-request@archie.mcgill.ca to join.

**Documents**

Deutsch, Peter. *archie - An Electronic Directory Service for the Internet*. [Available by anonymous FTP from host archie.mcgill.ca, directory /archie/pub, filename whatis.archie]

Deutsch, Peter. "Resource Discovery in an Internet Environment — The Archie Approach,' *Electronic Networking: Research, Applications and Policy*, 2(1) (Spring 1992): 45-51.

# BITNET

**What**

BITNET is a worldwide network linking computers of several hundred institutional members including colleges, universities, and collaborating research centers. BITNET (Because Its Time Network) refers to the combined constituent networks from the U.S. Mexico, Canada (NetNorth), and Europe (European Academic Research Network - EARN). Gateways exist between BITNET and the Internet, USENET, and other networks worldwide. BITNET is chartered for the purpose of facilitating noncommercial exchange of information consistent with the academic, educational, and research purposes of its members. Users share information via electronic mail to individuals and shared interest groups. Listserv software is used for distribution of mail and files from server machines. BITNET started as a small network of IBM computers at the City University of New York and is based on store-and-forward protocols (Network Job Entry/Network Job Interface - NJE/NJI). The links between nodes are required to operate at speeds of at least 9.6 Kbps. Members are also required to provide, without charge, at least one port to which another Member or Affiliate may connect to gain connectivity to BITNET.

**Who**

In 1989 CSNET and BITNET merged and officially became the Corporation for Research and Educational Networking (CREN), though the network is still largely referred to as BITNET. EDUCOM, a nonprofit consortium for information technology in higher education, provides overall management of CREN. Contact: CREN Information Center, Suite 600, 1112 Sixteenth Street, NW, Washington, D.C. 20036, 202-872-4200.

**For More Information**

### Electronic
The file NETINFO FILELIST available from the server LISTSERV@BITNIC contains an index of online information from the BITNET Information Center (BITNIC). This information includes policy documents, node information, newsletters, protocol documents, and help files. To retrieve the index, a request can be sent via email to LISTSERV@BITNIC and should contain the following as the only line in the body of the message:

```
send netinfo filelist
```

# Freenets

**What**

Freenets are open-access, free, community sponsored and maintained computer systems. In an effort to make the system accessible and useful to a wide variety of people, Freenets maintain general purpose services, such as email, Usenet news, and online multi-user chat. They also maintain community specific services, such as the library and city government information available in Cleveland, where one of the largest freenets, the Cleveland Freenet, is located. Users may use dialup connections to gain access, although several freenet sites are now also available on the Internet.

Freenets are structured around "areas", which are referred to as buildings or centers, to create an electronic city motif. The electronic city houses buildings, which house rooms, which house message boards and other informational items. These groupings are purely for navigational purposes, in that they make it easy for users to find the information which interests them.

You may login to a freenet as a one-time visitor. However, anyone who wants to join a particular freenet should apply for a free account. A login id and password will be provided which will allow you to add messages, and to fully use their electronic mail and other services. Since registration is free, there's no reason to be a visitor more than once.

**Who**

In September of 1988 the Community Telecomputing Laboratory was established at Case Western Reserve University. It operates as an activity under the office of the Vice-President of Information Services, Dr. Raymond K. Neff. Its director, Dr. Tom Grundner, is the developer of St. Silicon, the Cleveland Free-Net, the National Public Telecomputing Network, and the concept of Free-Net community computing. For more information, contact:

> T.M. Grundner, Ed.D. - Director
> The Community Telecomputing Laboratory
> Case Western Reserve University
> 319 Wickenden Building
> Cleveland, Ohio 44106
> (216) 368-5121

**Where**

Prominent freenet sites include:
- Cleveland Freenet - telnet to any one of freenet-in-a.cwru.edu, freenet-in-b.cwru.edu, or freenet-in-c.cwru.edu
- Tri-State Online - telnet to 129.137.100
    login: visitor
- Youngstown FreeNet - telnet to yfn.ysu.edu
    login: visitor

**For More Information**

For more information about the National Public Telecomputing Network (NPTN), send an e-mail request to: info@nptn.org. Information is also available via anonymous ftp from host nptn.org (192.55.234.52), in the pub directory.

# Gopher

**What**

Gopher is a protocol and software package designed to search, retrieve, and display documents from remote sites on the Internet. It accomplishes this using the client/server model of users running "client" software on their local machines that provide an interface that interacts with remote "servers" or computers that have information of interest. In addition to document retrieval, it is possible to initiate online connections with other systems via Gopher. Users interact with Gopher via a hierarchy of menus and can use the full-text searching capabilities of Gopher to identify desired documents. Once an appropriate item is selected, Gopher retrieves it from wherever on the network it resides and (if it is text) displays it. The user may feel as if all the information available to Gopher resides on their local computer, when in fact Gopher is interacting with a large number of independently owned and operated computers around the world. Gopher client software exists for several popular computer operating systems.

**Who**

Gopher was created by a development team at the University of Minnesota Micromputer and Workstation Networks Center. The team includes Bob Alberti, Farhad Anklesaria, Paul Lindner, Mark McCahill, and Daniel Torry. They can be reached via e-mail at: gopher@boombox.micro.umn.edu.

**Where**

*Gopher software and documentation* can be retrieved via anonymous FTP from boombox.micro.umn.edu, in the pub/gopher directory.

*To try the UNIX Gopher client,* TELNET to consultant.micro.umn.edu and login as "gopher".

**For More Information**

### Electronic
The Gopher Usenet newsgroup *comp.infosystems.gopher* is a source of gopher information and discussion of gopher issues.

There is also an Internet mail reflector for Gopher news. Send a free-text request to *gopher-news-request@boombox.micro.umn.edu* to be added to the mailing list.

### Print
Alberti, Bob, et. al. *The internet Gopher protocol*. University of Minnesota Microcomputer and Workstation Networks Center, 1992. [Available from host boombox.micro.umn.edu, pub/gopher/gopher_protocol directory, filename protocol.txt or protocol.MacWriteII.hqx]

# HYTELNET

**What**

HYTELNET is designed to assist in reaching all of the INTERNET-accessible libraries, Freenets, CWISs, Library BBSs, and other information sites by Telnet. HYTELNET was originally designed as a hypertext-like tool specifically for users who access Telnet via a modem by direct network connection from an IBM compatible personal computer. There is now additionally a UNIX version that will also initiate connections to remote systems on the user's behalf.

The PC version of HYTELNET, when loaded, is memory-resident. Because it is a memory-resident program it should be called-up before you load your communications program. You may have it sit in the background until you need to find a Telnet address. To invoke the program one just hits the Control and Back-space keys and follows the directions. After reading the site information the program can be returned to the background.

| | | |
|---|---|---|
| Program size: | 16065 bytes | (HyperRez on disk) |
| Installed size: | 59680 bytes | for program, text, and links) |

**Who**

This useful program was created and is maintained by Peter Scott of the University of Saskatchewan (scott@sklib.usask.ca). Earl Fogel of the University of Saskatchewan wrote the UNIX version of HYTELNET ( Earl Fogel can be contacted at fogel@sask.usask.ca).

**Where**

The UNIX version of HYTELNET can be previewed by following these instructions:

1.     Telnet ACCESS.USASK.CA or 128.233.3.1
2.     login: hytelnet

This UNIX software is available by anonymous FTP from host access.usask.ca in the pub/hytelnet/unix directory.

**For More Information**

Various files of information about HYTELNET, as well as the program files, are available via anonymous FTP from host access.usask.ca, in directory pub/hytelnet. Check the directory with an "ls" command to find the latest version of the program. The HYTELNET files are archived using a ZIP utility, which means you must specify "binary" during your FTP session before transferring HYTELNET. To unarchive it, you must be able to "unzip" the file with PKUNZIP. PKUNZIP is available for anonymous FTP in the pub/hytelnet/pc directory. For specific instructions on using FTP, including a sample session of a binary file transfer, refer to the *Internet File Transfer (FTP)* section.

To get on a mailing list of directory updates, write to Peter Scott at scott@sklib.usask.ca and request to be added to the LIB_HYTELNET list.

# Internet

**What**

The Internet is a worldwide network of computer networks, all supporting a common suite of telecommunications protocols. This suite of protocols, presently the Transmission Control Protocol/Internet Protocol (TCP/IP) suite of protocols, defines how the disparate computers of the Internet should communicate and what applications are supported. The three basic applications defined by the TCP/IP protocols are electronic mail (Simple Mail Transfer Protocol or SMTP), file transfer (File Transfer Protocol or FTP) and remote login (Telnet). The Internet is currently in about 80 countries around the world, linking over 900,000 computers and serving millions of individual users.

**Who**

Because the Internet is comprised of cooperating but independent networks, no single institution governs the Internet. The Internet is administered by governing boards and working groups, most of which are administered by the Internet Society (ISOC). The Internet Society oversees the Internet Architecture Board (formerly the Internet Activities Board), its working groups and task forces, and accessibility policy statements. The Internet Society can be reached by e-mail at isoc@nri.reston.va.us or at:

> The Internet Society
> 1895 Preston White Drive - Suite 100
> Reston, VA 22091

**For More Information**

To get on the mailing list of the *Internet Monthly Report*, a summary of activities of various networking organizations comprising the Internet in the United States, send a message to cooper@isi.edu. Back issues of the *Report* are available for anonymous FTP from host nis.nsf.net, in the publications/internet.monthly.report directory.

A discussion of issues relating to the commercialization and privatization of the Internet takes place on the discussion list *com-priv*. To subscribe to this discussion, send a free-text request to com-priv-request@psi.com.

Bowers, Karen, et. al. *FYI on Where to Start: A Bibliography of Internetworking Information*. Network Working Group, Request for Comments 1175, August 1990. [Available by anonymous FTP from host ftp.nisc.sri.com, directory rfc, filename rfc1175.txt]

Comer, Douglas. *Internetworking with TCP/IP; Volume 1: Principles, Protocols, and Architecture*. Second edition. Englewood Cliffs, NJ: Prentice-Hall, 1991.

LaQuey, Tracy L. *User's Directory of Computer Networks*. Bedford, MA: Digital Press, 1990.

Malkin, Gary. *FYI on Questions and Answers: Answers to Commonly Asked "New Internet User" Questions*. Network Working Group, Request for Comments 1325, May 1992. [Available by anonymous FTP from host ftp.nisc.sri.com, directory rfc, filename rfc1325.txt]

Quarterman, John S. *The Matrix: Computer Networks and Conferencing Systems Worldwide*. Bedford, MA: Digital Press, 1990.

# LIBS

**What**  LIBS is software written for the DEC VAX VMS or the UNIX operating systems that serves as a menu-driven gateway to remote systems on the Internet. Through a hierarchy of menus, you can identify a remote system to which you wish to connect, and then initiate the connection from within the LIBS software. LIBS will then connect you to the specified system.

**Who**  LIBS was written by:

Mark Resmer
Director
Computing, Media, Telecommunications
Sonoma State University
1801 E. Cotati Avenue
Rohnert Park, CA 94928
(707) 664-2889
(707) 664-2505 Fax
Mark.Resmer@sonoma.edu

**Where**  To try out the LIBS software, TELNET to vax.sonoma.edu or 130.157.2.3 and login as "LIBS". If you like it and wish to mount it on your VAX running VMS or a computer running UNIX, you can retrieve the software via anonymous FTP to sonoma.edu, in directory /pub, filename libs.com for the VMS version, libs.sh for the UNIX shell script.

**Beginning Screen**

```
            LIBS - Internet Access Software v1.3.U (beta)
        Mark Resmer, Sonoma State University, February 1992

                        Based on data provided by
                Art St. George, University of New Mexico
                            and other sources


        On-line services available through the Internet

            1. United States Library Catalogs
            2. Library Catalogs in other countries
            3. Campus-wide Information Systems
            4. Miscellaneous databases
            5. Information for first-time users of this program


        Enter the appropriate number followed by RETURN

        Press <return> to exit

        Enter the number of your choice:
```

# Project Gutenberg

**What**

Project Gutenberg was created in 1971 to encourage the creation and distribution of English language electronic texts. According to Project Gutenberg, their electronic texts are free of copyright restrictions (certain titles may be limited to use within the United States). Examples of texts currently available include *Alice in Wonderland*, *The CIA World Factbook*, *The Federalist Papers*, *O Pioneers!*, and *Paradise Lost*.

**Who**

Project Gutenberg was begun and is led by:
Michael S. Hart
Directory, Project Gutenberg
P.O. Box 2782
Champaign, IL 61825
hart@vmd.cso.uiuc.edu
HART@UIUCVMD.BITNET

**Where**

Information about Project Gutenberg and its electronic texts are available by anonymous FTP from host **mrcnext.cso.uiuc.edu** (128.174.201.12) in directory /etext and its subdirectories. *Other sites* that mirror the Gutenberg files include:

| Host | Directory |
| --- | --- |
| oes.orst.edu (128.193.124.2) | /pub/almanac/etext |
| quake.think.com (192.31.181.1) | /pub/etext |
| deneva.sdd.trw.com (129.193.73.1) | /pub/etext |

**For More Information**

Information files on Project Gutenberg are available by anonymous FTP from host mrcnext.cso.uiuc.edu in directory /etext/articles.

# Requests For Comments (RFCs)

**What**

Request for Comments (RFCs) are a series of documents that serve a variety of purposes on behalf of the Internet community. RFCs are primarily used to define Internet standards, but there are also whimsical RFCs (e.g., RFC 968: "'Twas the Night Before Start-up"), glossaries (e.g., RFC 1208), bibliographies (e.g., RFC 1175), reports, statistics, surveys, and any other document of potential interest to network users.

Of particular note is a series of RFCs called FYIs (For Your Information). This series is intended to address topics of general interest. Selected FYIs include:

FYI 3　(RFC 1175)　FYI on Where to Start: A Bibliography of Internetworking Information

FYI 4　(RFC 1325)　FYI on Questions and Answers: Answers to Commonly Asked "New Internet User" Questions

FYI 10 (RFC 1290)　There's Gold in Them Thar Networks! or Searching for Treasure in All the Wrong Places

FYI 12 (RFC 1302)　Building a Network Information Services Infrastructure

**Where**

Primary FTP repositories of RFCs include:

NIC.DDN.MIL　　- in directory rfc, filename rfc<number>.txt

FTP.NISC.SRI.COM　- in directory rfc, filename rfc<number>.txt

RFCs are also availabe via e-mail by sending the message "send rfcNNNN" (where NNNN is the RFC number) to: mail-server@nisc.sri.com. To obtain the RFC Index, send the message "send rfc-index".

**Who**

Submissions for Requests for Comments should be sent to Jon Postel at POSTEL@ISI.EDU. Please consult RFC 1111 "Instructions to RFC Authors" for more information.

Requests for special distribution of RFCs should be addressed to either the author of the RFC, to NIC@NIC.DDN.MIL, or to NISC@NISC.SRI.COM.

**For More Information**

**Electronic**

To subscribe to a mailing list of new RFC announcements, send a message to RFC-REQUEST@NIC.DDN.MIL, asking to be added to the new RFCs mailing list.

**Print**

Comer, Douglas. "A guide to RFCs," in *Internetworking with TCP/IP; Volume 1: Principles, Protocols, and Architecture.* Second edition. Englewood Cliffs, NJ: Prentice-Hall, 1991, p. 441-475.

# SLIP (Serial Line Internet Protocol)

**What**

The TCP/IP protocol family runs over a variety of network media: IEEE 802.3 (ethernet) and 802.5 (token ring) LANs, X.25 lines, satellite links, and serial lines. There are standard encapsulations for IP packets defined for many of these networks, but there is no standard for serial lines. SLIP is a *de facto* Internet Protocol (Serial Line Internet Protocol) used to run IP over serial connections such as telephone lines or RS232 cables connecting two systems. Though originally designed as an easy, reliable way to connect TCP/IP hosts and routers using serial lines, it has also been used for dialup purposes. Therefore it allows you to run Telnet, FTP, and other services from your local workstation or personal computer by converting a dialup session to another computer into a SLIP session.

**Where**

SLIP software is available both commercially and in public domain archives. Many of the Network Information Center (NIC) machines have SLIP software available for anonymous ftp. For example, versions of it that run on several different machines are available at nic.cerf.net in the /var/spool/ftp/pub/slip directory.

**For More Information**

You may want to read more about SLIP by reading the Request For Comments (RFCs - see the appropriate Fact Sheet) that pertain to it. Using FTP, look for RFC 1055 in any of the archives that maintain RFCs, such as ftp.nisc.sri.com. RFC 1055 refers to SLIP generically, as well as the 4.3BSD UNIX version.

# Usenet News

**What**

Usenet is a worldwide voluntary member network, with approximately one tenth as many nodes as the Internet. It is based upon the Unix-to-Unix Copy Program(UUCP), and is thus almost exclusively limited to systems that use the UNIX operating system. An open, distributed bulletin board and conferencing system is associated with Usenet such that all users can send messages and all messages can be read by all users. In the U.S. the conferencing is divided into over 1000 ongoing discussions called newsgroups. Each newsgroup refers to a particular topic and contains postings (often called articles) related to that topic and sent (or 'posted')to the newsgroup by individual users. Newsgroups are structured hierarchically by topic and subtopic. For example, the newsgroup sci.physics.fusion is a science newsgroup concentrating on physics discussions about nuclear fusion.

**How**

Unlike most other network services where data is sent across the network as a direct result of user instigation, articles are maintained on your local system first and later transferred between Usenet machines. When you invoke software to read or post articles you use a local database. Articles are not sent to individuals, thus reducing mail traffic within a system and local storage of redundant information. Articles to be distributed beyond the local system are collected and sent as files to adjoining Usenet sites. These sites in turn add their items and then forward them. In this way articles are propagated throughout the network usually within twenty-four hours.

There are many different pieces of software available for reading, sending, or replying to news. "Readnews" (abbreviated "rn") and "Postnews" (abbreviated "Pnews") are two that are widely used.

**Who**

You should check with your local system managers to see whether one of your institutional computers acts as a Usenet node.

**For More Information**

Much of the information about Usenet is available online. For example, the newsgroup mod.announce.newuser has helpful information for new users. In addition the following sources contain extensive information about USENET and newsgroups:

Rapaport, Matthew. *Computer Mediated Communications: Bulletin Boards, Computer conferencing, Electronic Mail, and Information Retrieval*. NY: Wiley, 1991.

Quarterman, John S. *The Matrix: Computer Networks and Conferencing Systems Worldwide*. Bedford, MA: Digital Press, 1990.

Todino, Grace. *Using UUCP and Usenet*. Fourth ed. Revised by Tim O'Reilly and Dale Dougherty. Newton, MA: O'Reilly & Associates, 1987.

# Wide Area Information Servers (WAIS)

**What**

WAIS (pronounced "ways") has been developed as a method to retrieve information from distributed databases on the Internet through a common interface. WAIS is a client-server system that utilizes the Z39.50 information retrieval standard. Hundreds of databases are available on the Internet to several WAIS client interfaces (Macintosh, XWindows, GNU emacs, simple shell, and a tool kit for making your own interface). Databases that can be accessed, searched, and displayed through a WAIS client include bibliographic databases, full-text databases, databases of various kinds of data (meteorological, astronomical, etc.), and many other types.

**Who**

Brewster Kahle of Thinking Machines Corporation is the project leader of the WAIS endeavor, but the primary contact for WAIS information is Barbara Lincoln:

> Thinking Machines Corporation
> 1010 El Camino Real, Suite 310
> Menlo Park, CA 94025
> (415) 329-9300
> barbara@think.com

**Where**

To try a simplified version of WAIS (through a much more primitive interface than is provided by using most WAIS clients), TELNET to quake.think.com and login as "wais". This interface is called "simple WAIS".

The FTP archive for WAIS software is on host think.com, in the /wais directory. The FTP location of the WAIS discussion, as well as other documents is on host quake.think.com in the /pub/wais/wais-discussion directory.

**For More Information**

### Electronic
There are several electronic discussions/mailing lists that discuss WAIS issues:
- wais-discussion@think.com is a weekly digest of mail from users and developers. To subscribe, send a message to wais-discussion-request@think.com.
- wais-interest@think.com announces new releases. To subscribe, send a message to wais-interest-request@think.com.
- wais-talk@think.com is a discussion list of WAIS developers. To subscribe, send a message to wais-talk-request@think.com.

### Print
Lincoln, Barbara. *Wide Area Information Servers (WAIS) Bibliography.* [Available online on host quake.think.com, directory /pub/wais/wais-discussion, filename bibliography.txt]

Markoff, John. "For the PC User, Vast Libraries," *New York Times*, (July 3, 1991):C1.

Stein, Richard. "Browsing Through Terabytes," *BYTE*, (May 1991): 157-164.

# World-Wide Web (W³)

**What**

The World-Wide Web (also knowns as "W³"), is a system being developed to provide hypertext access to documents wherever they are located (e.g., whether on your local workstation or a remote computer) via the Internet. It is based upon the client/server model of separating the user interface from the sources of the information. Therefore, the model is that the World-Wide Web user will use client software running on his/her personal computer that would serve as an information "browser" that is capable of making links to specific documents on computers around the world. Currently, a NeXTStep™ client is available, and browsing software for X11-based systems and Macintosh computers are being developed.

**Who**

The project leader is Tim Berners-Lee at CERN, the European Particle Physics Laboratory in Geneva, Switzerland. He can be reached at timbl@info.cern.ch.

**Where**

To try out the World-Wide Web, TELNET to info.cern.ch. The beginning screen is included below.

**For More Information**

Berners-Lee, T.J., R. Caillisau, J-F Groff, B. Pollerman, "World-Wide Web: The Information Universe," *Electronic Networking: Research, Applications and Policy* 2(1) (Spring 1992).

**Beginning Screen**

```
                                                      Welcome to CERN
The World-Wide Web: CERN entry point

   CERN is the European Particle Physics Laboratory in Geneva, Switzerland.
   Select by number information here, or elsewhere.

   Help[1]                  About this program

   World-Wide Web[2]        About the W3 global information initiative.

   CERN information[3]       Information from and about this site

   Particle Physics[4]       Other HEP sites with information servers

   Other Subjects[5]        Catalogue of all online information by subject. Also:
                            by server type[6]  .

   ** CHECK OUT X11 BROWSER "ViolaWWW": ANON FTP TO info.cern.ch in
   /pub/www/src *** Still beta, so keep bug reports calm :-)

   If you use this service frequently, please install this or any W3 browser on
   your own machine (see instructions[7] ). You can configure it to start
1-7, <RETURN> for more, Quit, or Help:
```

# Z39.50 Standard for Information Retrieval

**What**

Z39.50 is an American National Standard, or protocol, adopted in 1988. Work on this protocol began in the early 1980s and was developed by the National Information Standards Organization (NISO). International Standards Organization (ISO) draft standards 10162 and 10163 (called Search and Retrieve or SR) are the international counterparts.

Basically, two systems that both use Z39.50 can exchange queries and results and translate them into their native syntax. Thus a user can query a remote system while using the local, familiar command structure. Using Z39.50 a client system views a remote server's database as an information resource, not merely a collection of data. The standard allows the client to build queries in terms of logical information elements supported by the server. It also provides a framework for transmitting queries, managing results, and controlling computer resources. Because the communicating computers share an understanding of the data being selected on one machine and moved to another, Z39.50 is particularly suited to highly structured data such as bibliographic records. In fact it is the members of the library community who have been the primary designers and implementers of Z39.50. To date the most widely publicized and used adaptation of Z39.50 is by the Wide Area Information Servers (WAIS) project. (See WAIS Fact Sheet).

**Who**

Although the protocol is officially sanctioned by NISO there are several primary groups responsible for information about its use.

*Z39.50 Implementers Group*
Formed in March, 1990 and consisting of institutions and vendors interested in developing applications that use Z39.50. A listserv discussion list is maintained by this group, see below for subscription information.

*Z39.50 Maintenance Agency*
To organize experiences with and recommendations for the evolution of Z39.50 the Library of Congress was chosen as the "maintenance agency." Contact: Ray Denenberg of the MARC Standards and Network Development Office, Library of Congress, Washington, D.C.

**For More Information**

**Electronic**
The Z39.50 Implementers Group maintains a listserv discussion called "Z3950iw". Send subscription requests to LISTSERV@NERVM.NERDC.UFL.EDU

**Print**
Lynch, Clifford A. "Information Retrieval as a Network Application " *Library Hi Tech*, 32(4), 1990 pp. 57-72.

Lynch, Clifford A. *Z39.50 In Plain English: A Non-Technical Guide to the New NISO Standard for Library Automation Networking*. Third Edition. St. Louis, MO: Data Research Associates, n.d.

# H | Trainer's Aids

*This section contains:*

- Small Group Discussion Questions
- Checklist for Internet Trainers
- "Introduction to Networking" Overhead
- "What Are Networks" Overhead
- "Networks You May Have Heard About" Overhead
- Sample Access Pathway
- "Names and Addresses" Overhead
- Electronic Discussions Comparison
- Sample Documents from "Crossing the Internet Threshold"

# Small Group Discussion Questions

### Access vs. Ownership
To what extent does remote access to collections and information affect collection development, interlibrary loan, and resource sharing?

### Reference Organization
As reference personnel can increasingly be available to people who don't come in to the library, what impact will that have on the reference desk? What are the implications for staffing the desk?

### Training
Who is responsible for training staff? Training users? Should it be the library? The computer center? Should they share responsibility?

### Who Pays?
We know that network services are not free. As the government moves from a heavily-subsidized national network infrastructure to one provided and maintained privately, what will this mean for libraries and access to information?

### New Alliances
Librarians and systems professionals need to work more closely together. What other collegial relationships should we be establishing?

### New Communities
With computer networks, collaboration does not depend on geographic proximity. Who are your colleagues? How do you identify them? How does electronic collaboration affect scholarship?

### Professional Development
What counts toward professional advancement? To what extent can the peer review process be transferred to electronic arena. Do contributions to electronic journals count? Contributions to electronic conferences?

### Information Overload
Oh come on, these are obvious!

# Checklist for Internet Trainers

**Publicity**
Describe the content of the training program and the prerequisite skill level of participants

**Enrollment form**
Request information about enrollees (background, reason for attending)

**Instructor station** (test it beforehand)
- terminal capable of accessing the Internet
- computer projection equipment and screen
- podium
- writing equipment: easel/pad/pens; transparency projector/screen/blank transparencies/transparency pens; blackboard/chalk/eraser

**Participant stations** (if session is hands-on)
- terminals capable of accessing the Internet
- individual accounts/passwords that enable Internet access
- logon instructions by each terminal

**Handouts**
Paginate throughout, package in folder or binder

**Practice session**
- schedule a "dress rehearsal" for which participants are committed to providing a frank evaluation
- pay attention to the evaluation

**Support personnel**
- technical back up
- teaching aides to assist during hands-on exercises

**Basic costs**
- rental of computer-equipped room
- handouts: design, production, packaging
- honoraria for instructor(s)
- refreshments for breaks
- publicity: flyers, mailings, registration confirmation
- phone bills (including fax)
- name tags
- temporary computer center accounts/passwords for participants

# "Introduction to Networking" Overhead

Networking is a simple idea (the sharing of expensive resources between computers; communication between computer users)

made very complex in implementation.

Networking and the Internet have been described using several metaphors:

as a highway system - "cruising the Internet"
as an ocean - "navigating the Internet"
as special dwelling place - "crossing the Internet threshold"

Networks can be considered from (at least) these three perspectives:

Technological - How does it work?

Social / Political - Who makes it work?

Functional - What can be done?

Vocabulary we'll cover:

INTERNET — - international network of networks based on the TCP/IP protocol
BITNET — - cooperative education and research network, primarily provides email services
TCP/IP — - the protocol suite or set of rules for software and users to follow for networking within the Internet
EMAIL — - electronic mail: messaging services between computer users
LISTSERV — - BITNET service providing distributed messages that form conferences
TELNET — - Internet service providing connection ("remote logon") to a remote computer
FTP — - File Transfer Protocol allows moving files from one computer to another
ARCHIVE — - computer system which stores files for distribution
E-TEXT — - the full-text of a document available in electronic format (often through FTP)
E-SERIAL — - a periodical distributed in electronic form
IP ADDRESS — - a specially formulated number assigned to Internet computers e.g. "31.1.0.11"
NAME or NODE - a textual alias for a computer's IP Address e.g. "melvyl.berkeley.edu"; also known as Hostname or Nodename
USER NAME or ID - address representing a personal account on a computer, e.g., "jlo-lis@cmsa.berkeley.edu"

# "What Are Networks?" Overheads

| | Generic Categorization | Sample Entities | Units or vocabulary used to characterize |
|---|---|---|---|
| **Technological** | Hard (machines) | multiplexers, routers, gateways, cable types | number of machines, nodes or nets, speed - Kbps Mbps Gbps |
| | Soft (rules agreements) | OSI or TCP/IP protocols, local rules | Membership groups, informal groups, individuals |
| **Social/Political** | Users | PACS-L members | Conferences, Informal groups |
| | Standards Makers | ISO, ANSI, NISO, ALA, MARBI | Official bodies, Industry and de facto |
| | System Admins. | LAN, Campus, Conference moderators | Organizational units ("IS&T"), Prof. Organizations |
| | Documentors/Evaluators | Network Information Centers, John Quarterman, Art St. George | "RFC"s, ALA's Machine Assisted Reference Section |

**Functional**

| | | |
|---|---|---|
| Messaging | SMTP | Number of messages<br>message delay<br>sender/receiver address |
| File Exchange | FTP | Size of files<br>File location<br>"anonymous FTP" |
| Remote Login | TELNET<br>MELVYL "Gateway" | Host<br>Client<br>address |

# "Networks You May Have Heard About" Overhead

UUCP
JANET
EARN
etc.

BITNET

  - One network - academic and research institutions

  - Limited functions, limited members

  - Different (not TCP/IP) protocols

Internet

  - Network of networks

  - TCP/IP protocols

  - Origins in DARPA

  - World-wide connectivity

  - "real time" interactions

  - Three important functions
        - e-mail
        - file transfer
        - remote login

# Sample Access Pathway

A user at UC Berkeley may dial-in (A) or be directly connected to the Internet (B). Access to the remote database at Dartmouth (using Telnet) is routed through intervening networks.

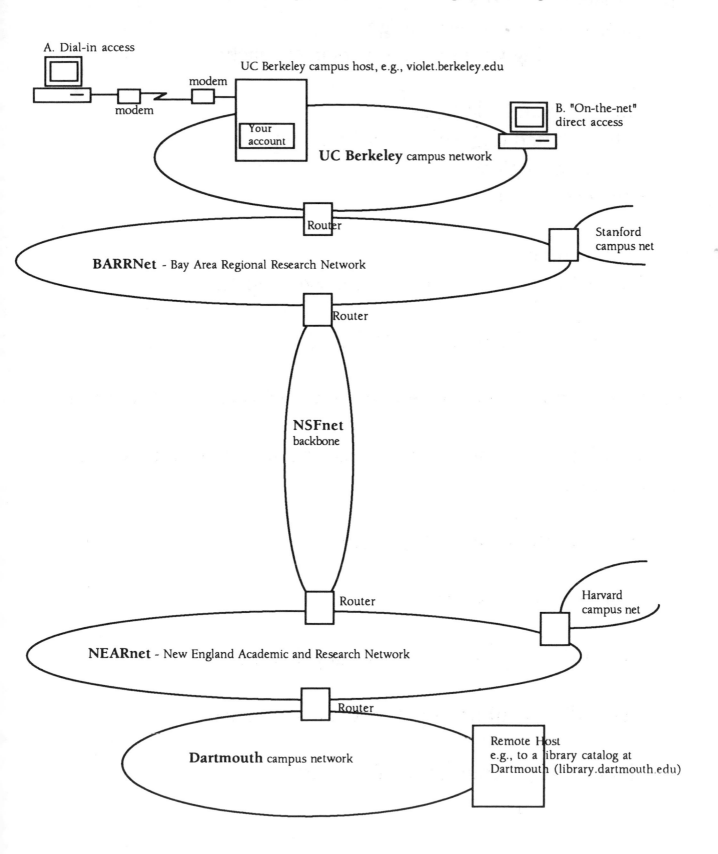

Note for trainers: This diagram, or one adapted to your local situations, can be drawn while explaining *inter*networking concepts.

# "Names and Addresses" Overhead

Appropriate metaphors:
    Getting to where you want to go
    Communicating with the right person or machine

Types of names and addresses:
    - protocol based (e.g. ethernet vs. internet)
    - physical vs. logical
    - person vs. machine

Internet machines
    - "names" are logical or textual: melvyl.ucop.edu

    - IP addresses are numeric: 31.1.0.11

Addresses and names are based on "domains" (i.e. are hierarchical)

Textual addresses arranged from most specific/smallest unit to most general/largest

      user@machine.network.domain

      user - account (person?)

      machine - e.g. "melvyl" - locally determined

      network - or subnet, e.g. "berkeley" - assigned

      domain - e.g. "com" or "edu" - assigned

# Electronic Discussions Comparison

|  | To Subscribe | To Participate |
|---|---|---|
| **LISTSERV Lists**<br>(usually BITNET-based) | Send the message "SUB <list name> <your name>" to LISTSERV@<list node> | Send e-mail to <list name>@<list node> |
| **Mail reflectors**<br>(usually Internet-based) | Send a free-text request to <list name>-request@<list domain> | Send e-mail to <list name>@<list domain> |
| **Usenet News** | You do not subscribe, but it requires some local administration | Use the appropriate post or reply news command |

Example of program agenda for hands-on workshop

**CROSSING THE INTERNET THRESHOLD: A HANDS-ON WORKSHOP**

**Session A: Thursday, June 25, 1992**
**University of California, Berkeley**

| | |
|---|---|
| 7:30-7:45am | Registration          *Location: The Faculty Club, Lewis Latimer Room* |
| 7:45-8:45am | Breakfast<br>Discussion: "Envisioning the impact of electronic networking on libraries" |
| 9:00am-noon<br>John Ober<br><br><br><br>Roy Tennant | Instruction          *Location: Room 211 Wheeler*<br>Overview<br> Networks in general, the Internet in particular, addresses and addressing<br> Demonstration of e-mail and conferences, remote login, and file transfer<br>Break<br>**E-mail and conferencing** |
| 12:15-1:15 | Lunch                    *Location: The Faculty Club, Lewis Latimer Room*<br>Discussions:   Pick from "Discussion Issues: (See *Crossing*..., p. H1)<br>                        or "Advanced Technical Issues" |
| 1:30-4:30pm<br>John Ober<br><br>Roy Tennant | Instruction          *Location: Room 211 Wheeler*<br>**Telnet**<br>Break                    Exercise leader: Anne Lipow<br>**FTP**                     assisted by: Laine Farley<br>How to keep up                        Stephanie Lipow<br>Extended Services<br>Windup |
| Supper hour | You're on your own.<br>Save room for hors d'oeuvres and dessert! |
| 7:00-9:00pm | *Note: Session B participants join Session A*<br><br>**Keynote address**     *Location: The Faculty Club, Library (upstairs)*<br>**Clifford Lynch**<br>**"Networking: The Near and Distant Future"**<br><br>**Reception follows**<br><br>(Session A participants complete an evaluation form) |

**Excerpts from pre-workshop mailing to participants in June 1992 hands-on workshop**

*A mailing to registrants confirming their enrollment contained a letter of welcome, a map showing the location of the workshop, a preliminary workshop schedule, and the following:*

## RSVP: Request for skill level

So that the instructors can prepare the workshop content and exercises appropriate to your needs, please return this form by [*date prior to the workshop*] indicating your skill level.

☐ Freshman  I got an Internet account too recently to have used it all; or, I've used only internal e-mail; or, I've used only personal e-mail to correspond with people outside my organization.

☐ Sophomore  I primarily use e-mail and subscribe to discussion groups. I've little to no experience using telnet or ftp.

☐ Junior  I've used mail, telnet, and ftp services, but don't feel that I know what I'm doing, nor can I independently solve problems when I run into them. I lack a conceptual framework for understanding what is happening.

☐ Senior  (a) I'm a frequent user of e-mail, telnet, and ftp, as well as navigating tools such as WAIS, but lack the technical information about the workings of the Internet. (b) I am attending mainly to get ideas by example about how to teach networking skills.

## Pre-workshop assignment for "freshmen"

If you have not yet subscribed to a listserver discussion group, BEFORE coming to the workshop, please subscribe to one of the 4 BITNET groups below; then, if you wish, unsubscribe a few days later. This will ensure a base level of experience among all participants. You may need the assistance of your local technical support staff to provide the proper protocol for BITNET addressing from your particular system. Whether or not you are successful, make notes about your experiences and observations.

*[A list of 4 discussion groups, their listserv addresses and topic focus followed; plus detailed instructions, with examples, for how to subscribe and unsubscribe.]*

# Sample Evaluation Form for Internet Workshop

*Your comments about what you found helpful and what would have made this program more useful to you will help in shaping future presentations. Use additional sheet for more space.*
*Thank you! --The instructors*

1. Overall, I found the workshop (circle a number):

          1   2   3   4   5   6   7   8   9  10
not worthwhile |-----|-----|-----|-----|-----|-----|-----|-----|-----|very worthwhile

  Please explain:

---

2. In particular, I liked the following:

---

3. <u>Given the one-day length</u>, how could the workshop have been more useful to you? What to drop? change?

---

4. Please assess the following aspects of each segment:

|  | confusing<br>uninteresting | clear<br>interesting |
|---|---|---|
| **A/OVERVEW** | 1  2  3  4  5  6  7  8 | 9  10 |
| Content | |-----|-----|-----|-----|-----|-----|-----|-----|-----| |
| Instructor (Ober) | |-----|-----|-----|-----|-----|-----|-----|-----|-----| |

    Please explain:_____

_____

|  | confusing<br>uninteresting | clear<br>interesting |
|---|---|---|
| **B/E-MAIL** | 1  2  3  4  5  6  7  8 | 9  10 |
| Content | |-----|-----|-----|-----|-----|-----|-----|-----|-----| |
| Instructor (Tennant) | |-----|-----|-----|-----|-----|-----|-----|-----|-----| |
| Exercise (Lipow) | |-----|-----|-----|-----|-----|-----|-----|-----|-----| |

    Please explain:_____

_____

_____

*(Continued on other side)*

**C/TELNET**

confusing / uninteresting ... clear / interesting

|               | 1 | 2 | 3 | 4 | 5 | 6 | 7 | 8 | 9 | 10 |
|---------------|---|---|---|---|---|---|---|---|---|----|
| Content       | \|-----\|-----\|-----\|-----\|-----\|-----\|-----\|-----\|-----\| |
| Instructor (Ober) | \|-----\|-----\|-----\|-----\|-----\|-----\|-----\|-----\|-----\| |
| Exercise (Lipow)  | \|-----\|-----\|-----\|-----\|-----\|-----\|-----\|-----\|-----\| |

Please explain:_____

_____

**D/FTP**

confusing / uninteresting ... clear / interesting

|               | 1 | 2 | 3 | 4 | 5 | 6 | 7 | 8 | 9 | 10 |
|---------------|---|---|---|---|---|---|---|---|---|----|
| Content       | \|-----\|-----\|-----\|-----\|-----\|-----\|-----\|-----\|-----\| |
| Instructor (Tennant) | \|-----\|-----\|-----\|-----\|-----\|-----\|-----\|-----\|-----\| |
| Exercise (Lipow)     | \|-----\|-----\|-----\|-----\|-----\|-----\|-----\|-----\|-----\| |

Please explain:_____

_____

**E. Keynote (Lynch)**   1 2 3 4 5 6 7 8 9 10

uninteresting \|-----\|-----\|-----\|-----\|-----\|-----\|-----\|-----\|-----\| interesting

**F/Handbook**

confusing / not useful ... clear / very useful

1 2 3 4 5 6 7 8 9 10

\|-----\|-----\|-----\|-----\|-----\|-----\|-----\|-----\|-----\|

Please explain:_____

_____

---

5. What I would really like to say is:

---

6. I <u>would</u> / <u>would not</u> recommend this workshop to others.
   (circle one)

---

7. Your Internet skill level...
   a. before this workshop: ☐ freshman  ☐ sophomore  ☐ junior  ☐ senior

   b. after this workshop: ☐ freshman  ☐ sophomore  ☐ junior  ☐ senior

Name_____ Affiliation_____

☐ *Check here if you use additional sheet for continuation or additional comments.*

# I | Appendix

*This section contains:*

- Networks Connected to NSFNET Backbone
- BARRNet Backbone Typology
- BARRNet Network Map
- NEARnet Geographical Map
- NEARnet Network Typology
- "Project to Analyze Internet Information..."
- "An Internet Reference Library"

# Networks Connected to the NSFNET Backbone

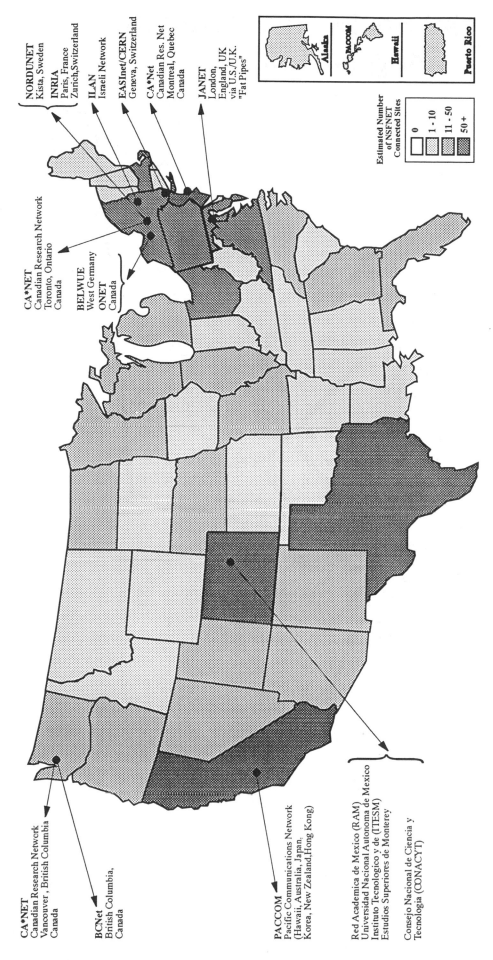

**CA*NET**
Canadian Research Network
Vancouver, British Columbia
Canada

**BCNet**
British Columbia,
Canada

**PACCOM**
Pacific Communications Network
(Hawaii, Australia, Japan,
Korea, New Zealand, Hong Kong)

Red Academica de Mexico (RAM)
Universidad Nacional Autonoma de Mexico
Instituto Tecnologico y de (ITESM)
Estudios Superiores de Monterey

Consejo Nacional de Ciencia y
Tecnologia (CONACYT)

**CA*NET**
Canadian Research Network
Toronto, Ontario
Canada

**BELWUE**
West Germany
**ONET**
Canada

**NORDUNET**
Kista, Sweden

**INRIA**
Paris, France
Zurich,Switzerland

**ILAN**
Israeli Network

**EASInet/CERN**
Geneva, Switzerland

**CA*Net**
Canadian Res. Net
Montreal, Quebec
Canada

**JANET**
London,
England, UK
via U.S./U.K.
"Fat Pipes"

Alaska

Hawaii

Puerto Rico

**Estimated Number
of NSFNET
Connected Sites**

| | |
|---|---|
| ☐ | 0 |
| | 1 - 10 |
| | 11 - 50 |
| | 50 + |

| STATE | SERVICE PROVIDERS |
|---|---|
| **Alabama** | SURAnet |
| **Alaska** | NorthWest Net |
| **Arizona** | Westnet |
| **Arkansas** | MIDnet |
| **California** | BARRNet, CERFnet, CSUnet, SDSCnet, Los Nettos |
| **Colorado** | CO Supernet, Westnet |
| **Connecticut** | NEARnet |
| **Delaware** | SURAnet |
| **District of Columbia** | SURAnet |
| **Florida** | SURAnet |
| **Georgia** | SURAnet |
| **Hawaii** | PACCOM |
| **Idaho** | MIDnet, NorthWestNet, Westnet |

| STATE | SERVICE PROVIDERS |
|---|---|
| **Illinois** | CICNet, INet, netIllinois |
| **Indiana** | CICNet |
| **Iowa** | CICNet, MIDnet |
| **Kansas** | MIDnet |
| **Kentucky** | SURAnet |
| **Louisiana** | SURAnet |
| **Maine** | NEARnet |
| **Maryland** | SURAnet |
| **Massachusetts** | NEARnet |
| **Michigan** | CICNet, Merit/MichNet |
| **Minnesota** | CICNet, MRNet |
| **Mississippi** | SURAnet |
| **Missouri** | MIDnet |
| **Montana** | NorthWestNet |

| STATE | SERVICE PROVIDERS |
|---|---|
| **Nebraska** | MIDnet |
| **Nevada** | NevadaNet |
| **New Hampshire** | NEARnet |
| **New Jersey** | JvNCnet |
| **New Mexico** | Westnet |
| **New York** | NyserNet |
| **North Carolina** | CONCERT, SURAnet |
| **North Dakota** | NorthWestNet |
| **Ohio** | CICNet, PSCnet, OARnet |
| **Oklahoma** | MIDnet |
| **Oregon** | NorthWestNet |
| **Pennsylvania** | PSCNET, PREPnet |
| **Puerto Rico** | SURAnet |
| **Rhode Island** | NEARnet |

| STATE | SERVICE PROVIDERS |
|---|---|
| **South Carolina** | SURAnet |
| **South Dakota** | MIDnet |
| **Tennessee** | SURAnet |
| **Texas** | SESQUINET, THEnet |
| **Utah** | Westnet |
| **Vermont** | NEARnet |
| **Virginia** | SURAnet, VERnet |
| **Washington** | NorthWestNet |
| **West Virginia** | PSCnet, SURAnet, WVNET |
| **Wisconsin** | CICnet, WiscNet |
| **Wyoming** | NorthWestNet, Westnet |
| **National and International Service Providers** | |
| Alternet, ANS, ICM, JvNCnet, PSInet | |

1/1992

# BARRNet Backbone Topology
# August 1992

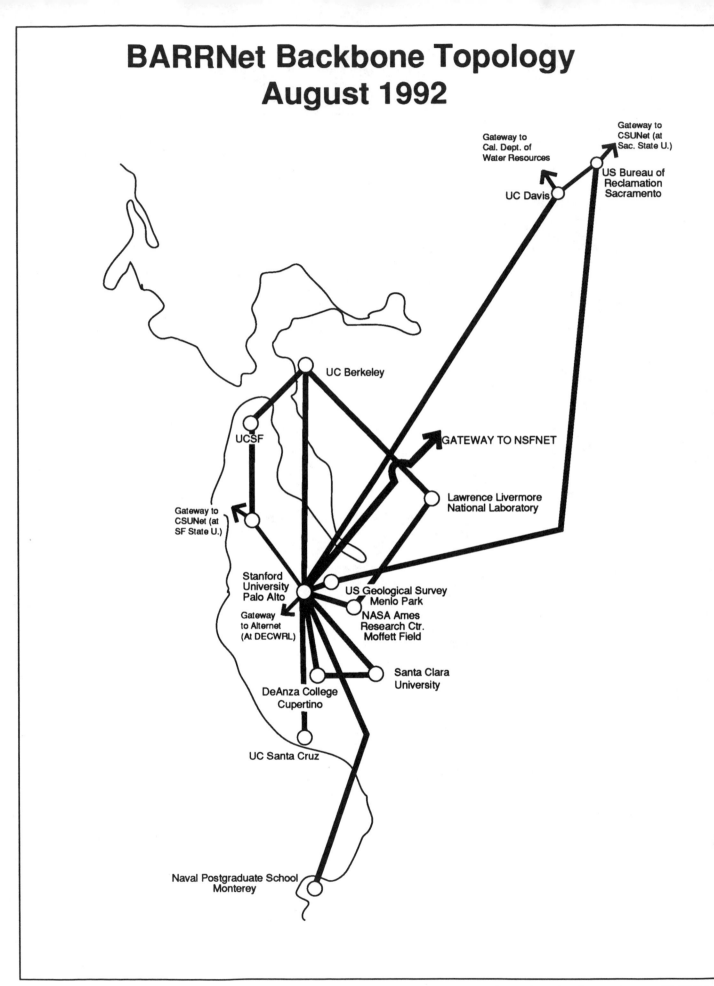

# BARRNet Network Map

NIC.BARRNET.NET:~ftp/barrnet/barrnet.ps

2 June 1992

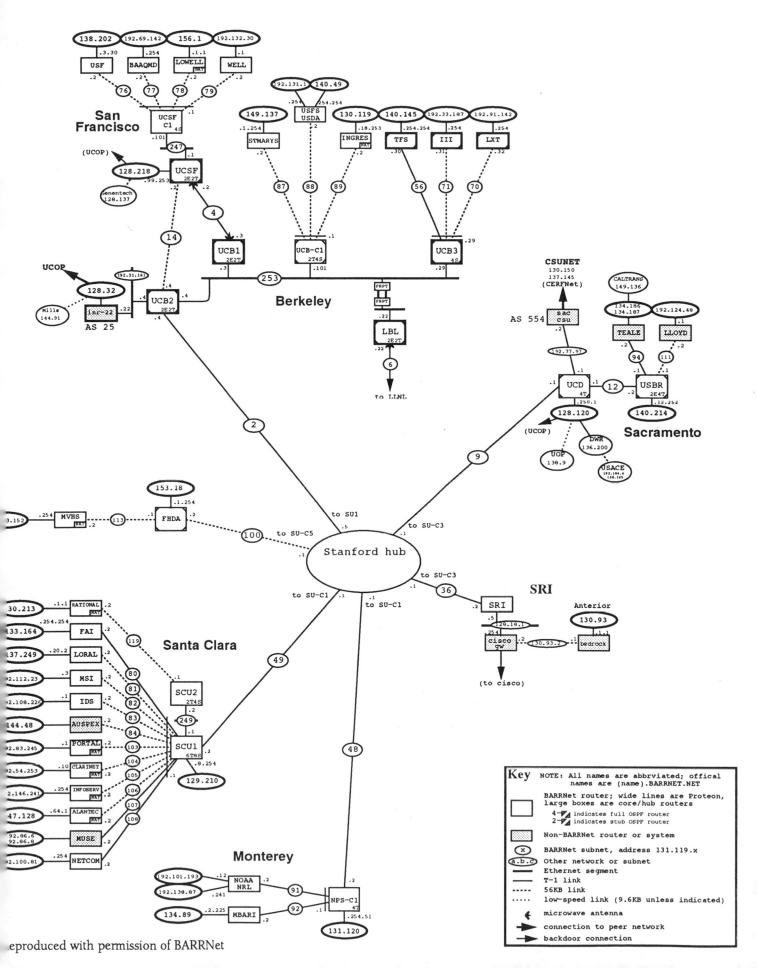

eproduced with permission of BARRNet

# NEARnet geographical map

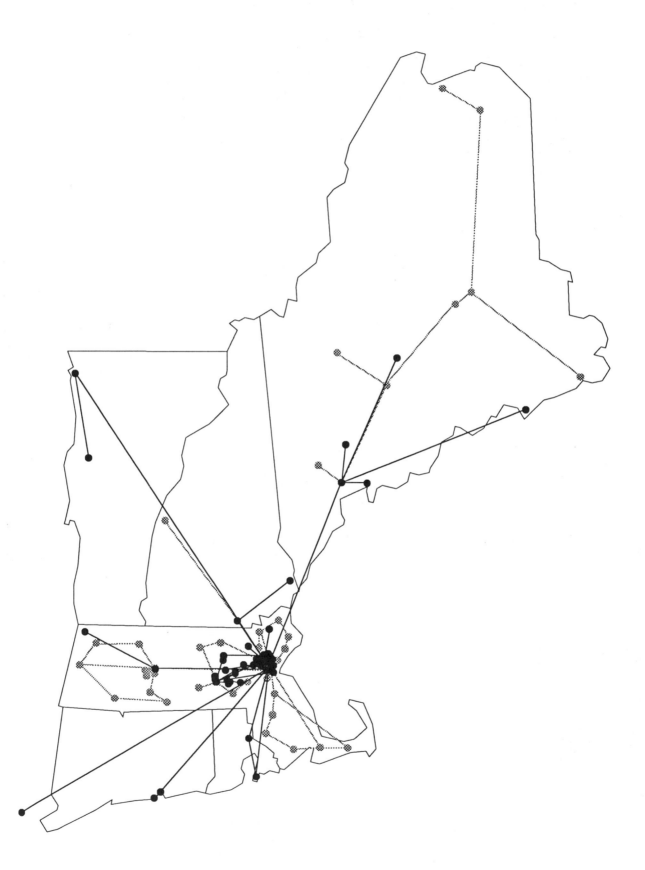

# NEARnet NETWORK TOPOLOGY

## as of

## June 25, 1992

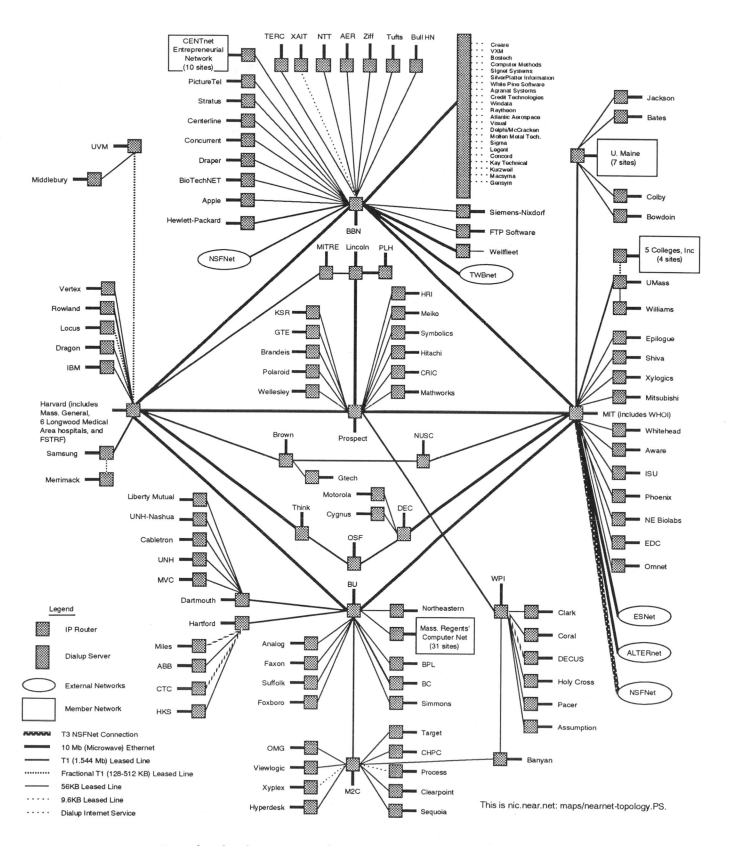

Reproduced with permission of NEARnet BBN Systems and Technology

# Project to analyze Internet information is under way

*by Erik Jul*

The OCLC Office of Research, with funding from the U.S. Department of Education, Library Programs, is currently investigating the nature of electronic textual information available via the Internet in a project titled Assessing Information on the Internet: Toward Providing Library Services for Computer-Mediated Communication. Here is an overview of the project's objectives and methods, preliminary findings, and a description of remaining work.

## Background

Locating, accessing, and using information resources on the Internet can be difficult, time-consuming, and sometimes impossible. In this new and rapidly developing electronic network environment, users have unprecedented access to information and computing resources. However, the development and implementation of systematic methods of describing and providing access to information lag behind deployment of the Internet itself, and the ability for network users to share information surpasses by far the ability to discover information on the Internet. Traditional library services such as cataloging have yet to find widespread application in this environment.

## Objective

The primary objective of this project is to provide an empirical analysis of textual information on the Internet that will inform the efforts of those interested in cataloging or otherwise describing and providing access to electronic resources in a wide-area network environment.

## Methods

Project methods include locating, collecting, and analyzing a sample of textual information on the Internet; developing and testing a taxonomy of electronic information based on the sample; and identifying and analyzing problems associated with cataloging, indexing, and providing appropriate levels of access to this information.

## Document Collection

During the early stages of the project, the focus has been to collect sample text documents from various Internet sources. Project staff use an array of resources to discover the whereabouts of electronic text, including printed books, journal articles, and newsletters; online electronic publications and lists; information discovery tools such as WAIS (Wide Area Information Server) by Thinking Machines Corporation, Gopher by the University of Minnesota, and Archie by McGill University; hypertext programs such as Hytelnet by Peter Scott of the University of Saskatchewan Library; electronic conferences; e-mail; and online browsing.

Using the primary Internet and BITNET protocols (file transfer, remote login, and e-mail), project staff have collected approximately 1,200 text documents from various Internet sources including File Transfer Protocol (FTP) sites, LISTSERV hosts, and interactive mail applications. For preliminary administrative purposes, the files have been separated into some 56 categories ranging from books and electronic journals to informal personal communications. (Although e-mail is beyond the scope of this project, some text files residing in publicly accessible directories are e-mail messages that have been saved. Determining this before retrieving the file is often impossible.)

The initial document collection was created as the result of directed searching, i.e., one document or information source would point to another. This introduces a bias into the collection, but does not prohibit preliminary analyses. To reduce the bias, a second collection will be gathered using automated methods developed by project staff.

## Preliminary Analysis

One hundred documents from the collection have been selected for preliminary manual analysis. Information gained during this phase will assist development of software to perform automated document analyses.

Project staff examined each document to determine its characteristics and create a simple cataloging record. Not surprisingly, the completeness of information useful for cataloging the documents ranged greatly. Some electronic journals, for example, provided considerable descriptive data, including ISSNs (International Standard Serials Number), whereas other documents had little or no descriptive elements.

Of the hundred documents, 96 provided some sort of information at the head of the file, before the text proper; 30 included additional information at the end of the file, following the text proper. Ninety documents had an identifiable title, but only 73 had an identifiable author. Fewer yet, only 64, had any kind of date within the text of the document.

## Cataloging Initiative

Project staff are presently expanding the cataloging portion of this project. A natural next step is to apply the existing MARC (MAchine-Readable Cataloging) Format for Computer Files to the documents in the collection. This exercise will reveal how effectively this format handles a broad range of electronic textual information and will simultaneously reveal the degree to which these electronic-text documents provide sufficient data for systematic cataloging.

> *"... the ability for network users to share information surpasses by far the ability to discover information ..."*

OCLC Newsletter   March/April 1992

The project staff, in coordination with professional catalogers and standards groups such as the Library of Congress and MARBI, will extend the cataloging initiative to discover the degree to which cataloging requirements are satisfied, through repeated application of the MARC Computer Files format over a wide range of documents.

Project findings are expected to assist standards organizations and others interested in providing systematic access to electronic information in a wide-area network environment. For more information or to receive a project report upon publication, contact me at (614) 764-4364 or kj@rsch.oclc.org.—Erik Jul is Communications Manager, OCLC Office of Research.

## Document Categories

| | |
|---|---|
| Abstracts | Statements |
| Directories | Briefs |
| Lists | Fact Sheets |
| Quotations | Poetry |
| Announcements | Summaries |
| Documentation | Brochures |
| Lyrics | Glossaries |
| Readme Files | Policies |
| Articles | Surveys |
| Drafts | Bulletins |
| Manuals | Guides |
| Recommenda- | Press Releases |
| tions | Theses |
| Bibliographies | Charters |
| E-Mail | Hearings |
| Minutes | Profiles |
| Reports/Papers | Testimonies |
| Bills | Conferences |
| Editorials | Humor |
| Monthly Reports | Proposals |
| Request for | Tutorials |
| Comments | Dictionaries |
| Biographies | Indexes |
| Encyclopedias | Public Laws |
| Newsletters | Weather |
| Standards | Digests |
| Books | Journals |
| Essays | Publicity |
| Notes | Workshops |

## What is the Internet?

The Internet, a global network of computer networks, had humble, inauspicious beginnings. In hindsight, nothing less than an information renaissance began on Sept. 1, 1969, at UCLA when a Honeywell 316 minicomputer named IMP Number 1 passed information to three similarly programmed remote computers in California and Utah. This IMP (interface message processor) was built by a team of scientists working in Massachusetts under a government research contract, the product of many minds sharing a common vision of networked, computer-to-computer communication.

IMPs were the predecessors of what are now called PSNs (packet switching nodes). Packet switching is the electronic process that provides the foundation for modern, high-speed telecommunications and global computer networking.

In packet switching, information streams are separated into discrete packets, each carrying identifiers and a destination label. These packets can travel independently, sharing wires, coaxial cables, radio waves, and fiber optic cables with many other packets going to many other destinations. Upon arrival at their destinations, the packets are reassembled to form the original whole information stream. Both short messages and entire volumes can move in this chopped-up-then-reassembled manner. If a transmission line seems too busy or fails, the packets automatically bypass it, hurrying along to their destinations and finding their proper places in the original whole. Packet switching has boomed steadily since 1969 and is now firmly integrated in most business, industrial, academic, and government communication systems, where electronic transactions are swiftly becoming the norm.

### ARPANET

The original research which has led to recent unprecedented growth in telecommunications and networking capabilities was funded by the Advanced Research Projects Agency (ARPA) of the U.S. Department of Defense, and the resulting electronic network was called ARPANET.

Heavy traffic on ARPANET inspired development and standardization of a suite of efficient connector protocols, known collectively as TCP/IP. The Defense Advanced Research Project Agency (DARPA) mandated use of these protocols in 1983. In 1984, ARPANET was partitioned and MILnet was separated for military use.

The success of electronic networking coupled with widespread availability of computers during the 1980s led to unacceptable levels of network congestion. In 1985, the National Science Foundation established five supercomputer centers throughout the U.S. connected by a 56 Kbps (kilobits/second) backbone network. Other regional and mid-level networks, primarily serving research centers and academic institutions, connected to this backbone to achieve interconnectivity and access to high-speed, high-capacity lines.

In 1987, the National Science Foundation awarded a five-year contract to Merit Network, Inc., a consortium of the state of Michigan, IBM, and MCI, to manage the NSFnet backbone network. Merit has overseen the installation of new backbone links that provide transmission rates of up to 45 Mbps (megabits/second), and implementation of 1 Gbps (gigabits/second) testbed links has begun. In 1989, ARPANET was decommissioned and replaced by the NSFnet.

As of March 1992, 4,891 foreign, regional, state, and local networks are connected to the NSFnet backbone, and through these networks more than 177,000 computers and 4 to 5 million users worldwide are interconnected. This worldwide network of networks has become know as the Internet.

Successful cooperation on this new global electronic playing field among government, industry, academic, and research sectors has introduced new concepts in time, distance, collaboration, and access to information.

## NREN

For several years, Sen. Albert Gore Jr. (D-TN) has offered legislation and championed federal funding to develop and support expanded access to the Internet for research and educational purposes. Senator Gore likened the Internet to a super-highway system for electronic information and asserted that the federal government had a proper role in providing for a new national infrastructure.

The High Performance Computing Act of 1991, signed by President Bush in December, promises continued national investment in this information-sharing system. Its name will be changed to the National Research and Education Network, or NREN, when the enabling legislation is funded and the system opens to more colleges and universities, public libraries, schools at all levels, and the general public.

## Read More About It

Here is a short list of recommended sources for clear and comprehensive descriptions of the Internet, its applications, and its potential for societal betterment.

The entire issue of *Scientific American* (September 1991) was devoted to articles about the Internet.

A comprehensive directory of the Internet is John Quarterman's *The Matrix* (Bedford, MA: Digital Press, 1990).

Also of interest are:

Arms, Caroline R. "A New Information Infrastructure." *Online* 14(5): 15-22; 1990 September.

Brownrigg, Edwin. *Developing the Information Superhighway: Issues for Libraries.* Chicago, Ill.: American Library Association.

Carlitz, Robert D. "Common Knowledge: Networks for Kindergarten through College." *EDUCOM Review* 26(2): 25-28; 1991 Summer.

Fisher, Sharon. "Wither NREN?" *Byte* 16(7): 181-189; 1991 July.

McClure, Charles R., et al. 1991. *The National Research and Education Network (NREN): Research and Policy Perspectives.* Norwood, N.J.: Ablex Publishing Corporation.

Smarr, Larry L., and Charles C. Catlett. "Life after Internet: Making Room for New Applications." *Information Technology Quarterly* 10(2): 12-21; 1991 Summer.

■ The NSFnet T1 (1.544 Mbps) backbone network with regional nodes and connections as of September 1991. The T3 network now being installed (not shown) transmits data at 45 Mbps.

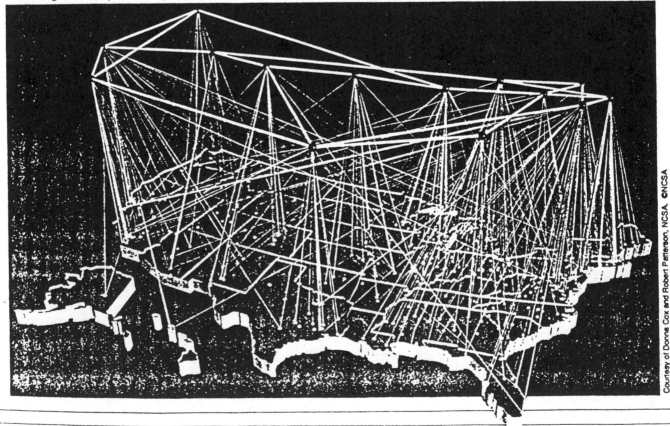

Courtesy of Donna Cox and Robert Patterson, NCSA. ©NCSA

The **MYND** of the **MELVYL**® System

* DLA news
* search tips & cautions
* teaching ideas
* questions & answers

# A forum for sharing information about the MELVYL System

Number 96, April 1992

**An Internet Reference Library.**

Many of us are becoming habitual users of the Internet and the dozens of online catalog systems to which it links us. Each of these systems is unique. In our early timid explorations, the most obvious singularity seemed to be the system interface. Now, as we become more comfortable with minor variations in dialect and even with significant differences in system presentation, it is the bibliographic content of the catalog and the value of its attendant resources which seem increasingly distinctive. And, increasingly those resources include not simply references to books and articles but also the contents of whole reference works, enhanced by electronic access to exceed the utility of their printed equivalents on the nearby reference shelves. So the Internet is no longer simply a virtual union catalog; it is becoming a virtual reference library. And since many of the titles in this library come in several versions, we can select the version which is most amenable to our searching style or information needs.

This issue of MOM lists several representative reference titles and their locations and provides a more detailed guide to one of the most useful resources, the CIA World Factbook, in three versions, each quite different in its character.

**Texts and Reference Books on the Internet.**

| Texts: | Systems: | Reference Sources: | Systems: |
|---|---|---|---|
| Bible | Dartmouth | Choice Book Reviews | CARL |
| " | Cleveland | Concise Oxford Dictionary | Rutgers |
| Book of Mormon | Cleveland | Environmental Education Directory | CARL |
| " | Rutgers | Internet Resource Guide | CARL |
| Dante | Dartmouth | Oxford Dict. of Familiar Quotations | Rutgers |
| Koran | Cleveland | Oxford Thesaurus | Rutgers |
| " | Rutgers | World Factbook | Dartmouth |
| Shakespeare Plays | Dartmouth | " | Cleveland |
| Shakespeare Sonnets | Dartmouth | " | Rutgers |

Thus, the 13 titles are mounted on 4 systems, of which 3 are menu-based: CARL (**use carl**); Cleveland Freenet (**use cfn**); and Rutgers (**use rutgers**). But these menu systems vary widely in their structures. CARL presents its resources in a categorical hierarchy, but both categories and resources are numbered in the same sequence (up to "69. Talent Bank."). Cleveland nests separately numbered choices inside a long succession of menus. Rutgers' Campus-Wide Information System lists well over 300 resources, unnumbered and ordered in the 18 screen outline in broad unexpected groupings (library resources are in the middle of the list, but "online reference material" is close to the end). The other, Dartmouth (**use dart**) is a command-based system very similar to our own. A close examination of the one title which appears on three systems illuminates that title, its triple treatment and the systems themselves.

MYND of the MELVYL System is edited by Alan Ritch, UC Santa Cruz, with the assistance of Laine Farley, UC Division of Library Automation, and distributed by DLA to all interested users of the MELVYL System. MELVYL is a registered trademark of the Regents of the University of California.

# A World of Information.

World Factbook is online in Ohio, New Jersey and New Hampshire. Which state should we go to and why?

## Use cfn.

Since Cleveland is closest, let's start with CFN. CFN's personality is chatty and reassuring. It tries to simulate a city, with clusters of information resources represented by urban locations. One of these, not surprisingly, is the Library (number 11 on the basic directory).
If you select 11 you see, among many other resources, "3. The electronic bookshelf."
When you select 3 you see, among several other titles, "5. The World Factbook."
When you select 5 you see, among a menu of features, "5. Read the World Factbook."
When you select 5 you see, on a list of geographical choices, "1. Nations."
When you select 1 you see a list of 14 alphabetical sections, of which "1." is "A."
When you select 1, you get ...
Well, by now, 7 menu levels into the system, as often as not, you have either
(a) lost your patience and typed "end, " to return to the MELVYL system, or
(b) lost your connection and been returned to the MELVYL system... so let's try New Jersey.

## Use rutgers.

Rutgers has an enormous menu of online files. These files in "outline" form occupy some 18 screens. Fortunately, you don't need to scan through all 18 to come to the section headed "Online reference material" with its four titles, the fourth of which is World Factbook. You can quickly discover the Factbook by entering "find" then, at the prompt, "world." This will not give you the "world" directly but it will show you the relevant menu items and their labels. To use the World Factbook itself, enter "goto" and then, at the "keyword" prompt, "world." You will then see the "word:" prompt. This is not, as you might assume, a free text index. Unless you enter the name of a country your search is likely to fail. If you do enter a country, you will see the Factbook article on your country, arranged by its many subheadings. Reasonably accessible, this presentation is not significantly more convenient than the display in the printed version. So let's try Dartmouth.

## Use dart.

Dartmouth, as we have indicated before, if not quite a MELVYL system clone, is our closest cousin. It's easy to get to any resource, including the Factbook (sel file world), and, when you get there, it's easy to use the command language. There are two indexes used with find: f cou [country] and f gen [any word]. But the real strength and flexibility of the dart version is in the versatile display formats. You can display complete data for a given country (d long), in a standard order of over 70 headings, including: climate; birth rate; literacy; suffrage; aid; currency; railroads; defense expenditures; and so on. Since this is likely to fill more than a dozen screens, you may prefer to display any of these sections, either individually (d rail) or in preselected clusters (d people, d economy, d geography) or your own groups (d religion ethnic).

What makes this a true electronic reference tool and not simply a page-turner is the gen index. Entering a term with f gen leads you to all occurrences of the term in any country. For example:
f gen emerald leads you to the two countries of the world which produce emeralds;
f gen ecowas finds the members of that African international organization;
f gen buddhis$ finds 21 countries with Buddhists in their populations;
f gen coca or cocaine finds 14 countries engaged in the production or trade of cocaine;
f gen muslim uranium finds 17 countries with Muslim adherents and that product; one of these is South Africa. To discover how many Muslims there are in South Africa you need a few display fields and a calculator: d population religion ethnic and then 20% of 2.8% of 39,550,000 = 221,480.
After a gen search the default display is the list of countries, but you can customize your displays to the countries and the contexts of the information.

So quite apart from the familiarity to us of the dart interface, that system's version of the World Factbook is clearly the most attractive version. In fact, even residents of Cleveland and New Jersey would be smart to point their own network antennae northeast, so inferior is their own access to the "World."

AR 4/92

# J | Index

# Index

44-98